COOKING IN MARFA

COOKING IN MARFA

WELCOME, WE'VE BEEN EXPECTING YOU

VIRGINIA LEBERMANN AND ROCKY BARNETTE
OF THE CAPRI

PHOTOGRAPHS BY DOUGLAS FRIEDMAN

Foreword
by Daniel Humm

Outside of my family and my restaurants, art is a driving force in my life. Art is my "input"; it feeds me, and then it allows me to feed others. Art, the evolution of an artist, and understanding the narrative that weaves through their body of work—these are such inspirations to me. Seeing the mark that one artist can leave upon the world always reminds me of the power that we have as individuals. In my somewhat frenetic life, I always make time for art; it seems like more and more these days my travels center on work I've been hoping to see and experience.

I've travelled to the desert before. I've made my pilgrimage to stand before and within Walter De Maria's mesmerizing and solemn Lightning Field. I've stood awestruck in the face of a life's work at James Turell's Roden Crater. These are life-changing must-visits. Next on my list was a return to the high plains, this time to the small and unbelievable thing that is Marfa, Texas.

I was fortunate enough to travel to Marfa my first time with my two of my closest friends, the artist couple Daniel Turner and Rita Ackermann, both of whom produced site-specific works for the renovation of our New York City restaurant, Eleven Madison Park. They each had a residency in Marfa, at different times in their lives, and they both felt a quite-deep connection to the place. They said, "Daniel, you have to come with us. We'll stay for a week." Everyone I spoke to thought I was crazy—a week? You could see everything there was to see in a day, I was told. Rita countered: "The thing that is most special about this place is the place itself. We will take it slow."

And she was right—Marfa was amazing; there is a somewhat spiritual and electric quality to it. The ethereal landscape and the candied, nearly-neon sunsets; the sense of community and creativity and the ever-present *how the hell did this all happen?* Thoughts of gratitude.

I found great art there, but I was admittedly not expecting a head-spinning, deliciously warm, creative meal that stayed with me long after I had gone. In the Capri, Virginia and Rocky have created a restaurant that is spectacularly the pure embodiment of its place. It cannot exist anywhere else. This is no small feat. The restaurant is special. Being outdoors by the open fire, spending time in the garden, being attended to in the most warm and caring way—that magical feeling of being in an extension of someone's home, not their business.

And the food! I had no idea I would encounter cooking like that: both rustic and beautiful, primal and refined, seriously executed but not taking itself too seriously. I learned that there could be a bounty out there in the desert. I learned that I had so much to learn about the ingredients, the people, the cuisine of the region. I felt satiated at the end (and a bit tipsy), and something else—refreshed.

The next day we went for a hike through Big Bend National Park. Rocky insisted we stop by in the morning before we left; he had a gift for us for our travels. He had prepared a set of margarita-making kits for our journey. It was that morning that I learned the concept of "the roadie." I nursed my slight hangover with the blazing sun beating down on me and a bit more tequila, and I smiled to myself. At my restaurant in New York, we give our departing guests a jar of granola to enjoy the next day—a way to lengthen the time they are in our care, so to speak. I love how Rocky and I both shared that desire but executed in our own ways.

I quite often catch myself reflecting on this incredibly special town and the perfect little restaurant that Rocky and Virginia have created here and that I am longing to return to. You have in your hands a passport of sorts, a window into their passion and creativity, and all of the wonders they are so good to share with us. I hope—I know—you'll be as inspired as I am.

Marfa, About a Mile High

Once you finally arrive after the long journey, the vast landscape, the quality of the air and light, and the sunsets change the rhythm of your perception. You can take a deep breath. Then you can start to understand the magnitude of the creativity and inspiration happening behind the crumbling facades.

THE SPACE BETWEEN

by Virginia Lebermann

In Marfa, it is the space between the clouds that always holds my attention. There is infinite potential that exists in the void between the visible or tangible. By focusing there, between the clouds, I find the clarity to conjure spontaneous and unexpected ideas. Out here you can drive for hours and often never see another vehicle. I find that thrilling. When you drive east to west, or vice versa, you ride parallel to an imaginary line, or rather, a river between two radically different cultures: Texas and Chihuahua, Mexico. The expanse of unobstructed light holds a twinge of romance from a distant land, a long time ago. It's the feeling that I'm living a story that was written in the past, when there were fewer stories to be told, the feeling that my footprint still matters—that's what keeps me here. There is perceived and real struggle to living in the middle of this austerity. I'm grateful for that struggle. It's visceral. I'm convinced that living in a less unusual place, a more convenient place, a path more easily taken, I would succumb to my lesser self. The side with the potential to be lazy and comfortable where I might quietly acquiesce to a life that does not transcend the ordinary. Marfa keeps me stretching and reaching for an explanation. A way to think about this place. A way to think about myself. It will never allow me to get comfortable. I like that.

When I came back to Texas full time in 2000, I did not yet realize that like my family before me, I would become immersed in the land, the history, the wildness, and the unique potential that Texas offers for existing on the edge—where one culture ends, and another begins. The edge of things, of culture, is what interests me. I had traveled a long way and for a lot of years to learn what that meant. Eventually, I understood that the perfect edge, the perfect vastness, and that certain provocative anxiety around your own uncharted potential existed right here, at home. It existed in this wily, unruly, unpredictable Chihuahuan Desert.

The Chihuahuan Desert spans from Northern Mexico to West Texas and parts of New Mexico and Arizona. It is the third largest desert in the Western Hemisphere and the second largest in North America. It spans state lines and national boundaries. Outside of urban clusters it is largely untouched by the visual repetition of corporate chain stores and restaurants that now define the perpetual landscape in this country. The town of Marfa sits on the high desert plains fifty-nine miles north of the Texas-Mexico border on Highway 67. This highway connects Marfa and Ojinaga, Mexico, our closest point of entry on the Mexican border to the south. The border, *la frontera*, is a culture all its own. In this instance, it is not exactly Texas or Mexico. It is a regional collision of vastly different yet intertwined histories, cultures, and economic and political structures. In this collision, there is a rich and graceful cultural symbiosis, albeit one that is often fraught with political tensions. There is no wall on this section of the border. The expanses of inhospitable desert and rough mountain terrain create their own natural barrier. It would be an incomprehensible feat of engineering to build a wall on our section of the border. The closest entry point to Marfa is about an hour away and consists of two towns: Presidio, Texas, and Ojinaga, Mexico. Both are small towns and the flow of people between the two countries is gentle and easy compared to the larger urban ports of entry like El Paso-Juarez, a 2½-hour drive west from Marfa. Ours is a rural landscape in the border region.

Though not directly on the Rio Grande, the river that creates the natural borderline between our two countries, Marfa itself is a reflection of both the symbiosis and tension between the countries: We work together here; we help each other. Yet there is a bubbling tension between the old and new, the true local and the newcomers, the cultures of the past and the cultures of the present, existing simultaneously. It keeps us all on our toes. A friend in Oaxaca recently shared this saying with me:

"*Pueblo chico, infierno grande.*"
"Small town, big hell."

To live in this small, sometimes fiery and contentious, community of Marfa it is important to respect the past, participate in the present, and think hard about how you might be affecting the future.

The interdependence among allies in a rural environment with few material resources is a unique relationship. It is delicate and it must be respected. If you stop getting along with the welder, it's almost impossible to find another welder. If you make the honey man mad, you will be left with commercial honey as your only remaining option. There are certain questions we don't ask people.

"Why did you move here?"

is one of those questions. You never know out here who might be on the lam from questionable situations back home. Or who came to the desert to reinvent themselves. We call this desert decorum. Let people's pasts be in the past unless they offer up the story without being asked.

There is a certain vibration, a certain pitch small towns possess, especially this one. It is tender and tumultuous. It requires a lot of patience and refines your ability to let go, to forgive and to ask forgiveness. It requires acceptance of many different truths and the refined ability to ignore transgressions. We hold each other up pretty well around here. Sometimes we support each other quietly and sometimes with grand gestures. It's a tough place. It is high intensity. It is filled with some big personalities, big characters, and strong opinions. Town is a tight space in a vast landscape. When the winds blow hard in the spring, people get crazy. When the dust storms envelope us for days, people get angry. But we are all we've got. There is little reprieve here. We make it work because this is where we have chosen to live. When we are gone, we miss it. We miss the people and the need for constant creative solutions to extraordinary problems where resources are slim.

A family member of mine has owned a ranch just south of Marfa since the 1950s and I've been in and out and through West Texas all of my life, though I grew up on the other side of the state, on the Texas Gulf Coast. My mother's people were multiple generations of Irish ranchers who had originally arrived in those coastal plains in 1834. They have, for seven generations, determined their own destinies and rules in a landscape of open and undefined potential. My great-great-grandfather came across the pond at age seventeen. He came to Texas with his uncle, who was working with the Mexican government to populate the northern region of Mexico, which is now Texas, with Irish Catholic immigrants. It was an orchestrated effort to expand Catholicism and maintain a religious stronghold of the church outside of Europe. Just after arriving he fought in the Texas Revolution and was subsequently a signer of the Texas Declaration of Independence. He was given a land grant for his bravery in the war. By running freight for the Republic of Texas, he was able to continue buying land and amassed a substantial ranch before his death. He set a course for generations of family ranchers, recluses, writers, oilmen, and eccentrics who would forever be tied to living a protected and relatively isolated existence on wide expanses of unpopulated land. In this tradition, just like my mother, I was raised to hunt, fish, ride horses, and work cattle. It was the life that most people imagine Texans live, but that in reality most don't. We are a stereotype.

My father came from a small town outside of Dallas, in North Texas. His was a structured upbringing inside the more controlled box of urban civility as opposed to the cultural and spatial freedom provided by life on the ranches. His father was the town doctor, surgeon, and mayor. His mother was the genteel hand that held all the familial parts together. My father was blinded in an accident at age twelve—he was "hard of seeing," as he used to say—and as a result his life was filled with a focus on the other four senses. Taste and, therefore, food and eating were vibrant and connective experiences for him. He filled his life, and our family life, with politics, literature, art, and music. We would spend hours at the most elaborate meals discussing the flavors of the food and wine. We talked about paintings, but he preferred sculpture. Yet out on the ranch where I grew up, we were riding pumpjacks in the night, racing cars across the pasture, drinking whiskey, and smoking cigarettes. With her wry humor, my mother would bring those two worlds of wildness and civility together by telling us,

> "Always know what the rules are so you can
> break them with grace."

Being raised between these two worlds prepared me, in fact encouraged me, to consider creating pools of civility in the middle of an untamed expanse of land and dust and wind.

I later pushed to expand my utterly Texan perspective, determined to shatter any convention of a provincial upbringing. I traveled aggressively most of my adult life. I wanted to know more of the diversity of human experiences, to feel the weight of cultures older and deeper than my own.

I sought to break the mold of being Texan and to create an identity encompassing layers of my own experiences outside the boundaries of the motherland of Texas.

In Nepal, at nineteen years old, I worked for a women's developmental art project in Janakpur on the southern border with India. The Maithili have traditional ceremonial murals that for centuries they have painted on the walls above their matrimonial beds. I worked with fourteen women to transfer this large body of symbolic and religious artwork from the walls of their homes to handmade paper, so they could be shown at the National Gallery in Kathmandu for the first time. These fourteen women were rattling the foundations of their small society by working outside the home, beyond family. Their audacity to earn money painting, to travel to Kathmandu without their husbands, and to engage in broader Nepalese culture at the National Gallery had made them outcasts. Through them I learned the incredible resilience it requires to forge new ground, break with tradition, and project your voice in a place where it has never been heard before.

In my twenties I spent time in Africa. There, I saw the romance of the vast landscapes untouched by the human hand. Sitting in those expanses of land I felt so very small and perfectly irrelevant. In the mayhem of cities, I feel fragmented, like I'm following someone else's course. In open spaces I have the strength to think about how to start from the beginning and hopefully stumble on something different. In Africa, people live life on a sharper edge than I had ever known. I slept under the stars with nothing more than a mosquito net. Predictably, I guess, in Africa anyway, lions walked through my camp one night. I didn't even have a sheet of tent canvas between me and that pride. All I had was a borrowed pistol and a wavering transparent mosquito net. Yet I felt astonishingly calm and that my twenty-seven years on Earth had been a good run. A gracious plenty.

Throughout my travels in Europe, I stood in the grandeur of the architecture. I was immersed in the work of the Renaissance artists. I read Homer. I did all the things you're supposed to do. But most importantly, I learned about the table and the art of conversation. They were long tables, some elaborate and others beautifully simple—in homes, gardens, and out in the countryside. Families shared stories about their traditional family recipes, their orchards, artwork, work, their intentions. They came together around a table to share the facts and expand on their dreams. Their life was lived around cooking and eating together. It is a pace and rhythm I admire. One that I hope we have brought to the spirit of our restaurant, the Capri. A place that grounds our guests in their community of friends and family around food, music and conversation. A place where memories are chiseled in stone.

Of all these experiences throughout my life, my travels in Mexico have always had the most profound reverberations for me. It's so close to home. It is a constant privilege to be near the reconstructed edifices of the Maya and Aztec—ancient civilizations of such elaborate sophistication and ingenuity—as well as to have the opportunity to experience the culinary traditions and ancient ceremonies of our neighbors. I was taught so little about these cultures throughout the normal course of education in Texas— they are rooted on the same landmass where we live, yet I was taught as if the man-made border between us and them had always existed. As an adult I started reading writers like Charles Mann and learned that trade and cultural communication existed between the ancient indigenous peoples of North America and Mesoamerica, and that the ruins of Paquimé—the northern-most center of trade for the Southern Mesoamericans for three hundred years—is just three hours south of El Paso by car. I was elated.

* * *

Despite all of my time away from Texas, I found the romance, the nostalgia, all the potential of the future existed, for me, in the open spaces, the broad landscapes, and the expansive skies of Marfa and the West. I am solid in vastness. In Marfa, I can garner that strength and hope to trip over a different, more unusual way of living. When I returned at the age of thirty, I saw it as a place where I could begin to build a legacy of my own—not entirely separate from family history but not right on top of it either.

In Marfa, there are two collaborations that have most specifically shaped my experience and helped me form my adult life. The first is with the formidable Fairfax Dorn, with whom I co-founded Ballroom Marfa, a contemporary art foundation focused on commissioning and exhibiting new works by artists, filmmakers, and musicians. Creating the Ballroom cultural arts space was my first creative endeavor in Marfa, and would solidify a path to expanding our cultural explorations through culinary experiments at the Capri restaurant just down the road from the

Ballroom building. Accordingly, the second collaboration of profound importance in my life is with Joseph Rockwell Barnette, my partner in the Capri. As a restaurant, the Capri is a culinary extension of Ballroom's work as a cultural laboratory. Both Ballroom and Capri have been our efforts in a broader cultural landscape to create space where people from diverse backgrounds can come together in conversation and creativity to deepen our understanding of ourselves, each other, the world we live in, the history we ride on, and the future we are creating.

Marfa makes sense as a home for these endeavors because it is a place where worlds collide. There are multigenerational families that were here when this was still Mexico, ranchers of European descent, artists, patrons, collectors, railroad workers, border patrol, fashion designers, builders, social workers, photographers, tomato factory workers, cultural travelers, intrepid travelers, and transient hipsters all existing in 1.6 square miles, at "about a mile high" with a population of 1,800 people, more or less. It is fundamentally populated by individuals and families who have been here forever. But it is also a transient society.

In the early 1970s, the Minimalist artist Donald Judd arrived in Marfa— long before the town was known to the outside world. Judd's name and work are inextricably linked to the story of Marfa. With the help of others, he created large-scale installations not only of his work, but also the work of many other artists, including Dan Flavin and John Chamberlain. He created the Chinati and Judd Foundations. Subsequently, since Judd's passing, his foundations have expanded their collections to include installations by Robert Erwin, Carl Andre, and many others. Donald Judd's story marks the beginning of Marfa being recognized as one of the most relevant art pilgrimages on the planet. People arrive every day of the week and most usually leave two to four days later. A striking number of those people are artists, filmmakers, writers, musicians, collectors, and curators. They have all traveled an immense distance to see Judd's work, or to write under the generous wing of the Lannan Foundation's prestigious arts and writing residency program. Others visit Marfa for readings and concerts produced by the Marfa Book Company, a literary hub for books, lectures, and music. Still others arrive to engage in the vibrant conversations between artists, musicians, and filmmakers creating shows at Ballroom Marfa. Our lives constantly intersect with these artists and writers. It has a profound impact on the intellectual combustion of our daily experiences in Marfa.

The town itself is an island surrounded on all sides by private ranches. As you arrive from any direction, it is the open ranch land you drive through that gives the journey its power and appeal. If you drive in from the east or south, you are required to push your way through a one-lane border patrol checkpoint. To the west of Marfa, on the south side of Highway 90, there is a US Customs and Border Protection blimp called the Aerostat, a tethered radar ground surveillance system. Its purpose is to support and provide information to the federal agencies involved in the nation's drug interdiction program. It is easy to drive through town without knowing or noticing why Marfa holds such a romanticized reputation around the globe. You could very well miss it altogether. It appears to be indistinguishable from so many roadside towns in the West. The only obstacle to slow your pace through town is a single four-way stop with a blinking red light.

Every day at high noon and six in the evening, the church bells ring. They are a reminder that lunchtime and dinnertime are upon us, respectively. We have one commercial general store called Dollar General. Its shelves are usually barren and disorganized. When I first moved here you had to drive twenty-six miles to buy a thermometer. There is never a line to vote at the county courthouse, and the only truly local festival, the Marfa Lights Festival, is a properly small-town ode to funnel cakes and airbrushed trucker hats. The Marfa public school mascot is the shorthorn, a breed of cattle that originated in England in the eighteenth century. During homecoming weekend, every road sign shimmers with the purple and silver mylar streamers of the Shorthorn football team.

We are a small town, just like so many others, with an unusual bubble of high art hovering in the air. They sell a T-shirt at the drive-through liquor store that says,

"Marfa: a drinking town with an art problem."

There are public receptacles for trash in town that are old oil drums painted red, white, and blue with the words,

"This Is Not Art"

painted around their circumference. It's difficult for people to grasp the layers of life in this town. Most who travel to Marfa are focused on their modern pilgrimage to high art. They don't realize this is a community, a town with its own history that long predates the art-world installations.

Marfa is still quieter than most creative strongholds. It is not as quiet as it was back when one survived only on corn dogs from the gas station and the town consisted mostly of tumbleweeds, very few cars, and infinite potential. In the beginning, we were drawn to the rhythm of the pilgrimage, the long drawn-out space of time it required to experience world-class creativity in the silence of a remote and precious landscape. It was tremendously exciting and strangely exhilarating. To experience art here has always been a unique counterbalance to the overstimulation of urban environments. You can still feel the work in a different and perhaps deeper context. Once you finally arrive after the long journey, the vast landscape, the quality of the air and light, and the sunsets change the rhythm of your perception. You can take a deep breath. Then you can start to understand the magnitude of the creativity and inspiration happening behind the crumbling facades.

WELL, HOW DID I GET HERE?

by Rocky Barnette

In the spring of 2007, my ladyfriend at the time told me we were going to visit friends in Marfa. To which I replied,

"What the hell is a Marfa?"

At the time we were living in Washington, DC, but we wound up visiting Marfa four times over the course of a year and fell under the spell that I have now seen countless couples and visitors fall under as well. You fall in love with the seeming dusty simplicity of the town, the ranchers, the Latino culture and proximity to Mexico, and the faint whiff of learnedness, academia, and artistic freedom blowing in the forty mile per hour breeze. That's when you start looking at real estate. Or at least we did. Not only that, I quit my job as the chef at a restaurant I loved; got a remote gig with a consumer advocacy organization teaching people about sustainable seafood, the farm bill, and water rights; bought a house in Marfa during the 2008 financial crisis because I couldn't get a loan for my dream taqueria; and became a Texas resident.

One year later, the ladyfriend had left, my contract was up with my job, and I found myself alone, unemployed, and a home owner in Marfa, Texas. The song "Once in a Lifetime" from Talking Heads sprang to mind. And I asked myself,

"Well, how did I get here?"

But I was dedicated to my new geographic location and eager to be a contributing member of my new community.

I originally came from Appalachia—Asheville, North Carolina, to be exact. Being born a bastard child, I had the great fortune of being partially

raised by my great-grandmother while my single mother worked. My great-grandmother's name was Evelyn Juanita Barnette; often when I feel ablaze with passion, I claim to be Mexican, citing her middle name as proof of my lineage. She and my great-grandfather lived in western North Carolina for the majority of the twentieth century and reaped the benefits of living through the Great Depression and every major war of that time; they raised almost all of their own food and knew how to cook it. When I was born they still kept their own hogs, had a massive garden, and ran their own produce stand on the side of the highway. They had an obsession with fresh fruits and vegetables that passed on to my grandfather, my mother, and me. Although my mother and I did not receive the green thumb part of the equation, my grandfather did, and at eighty years old he is still a grand-master gardener and even grows chiles every summer, which he dries and sends to us for use at the Capri. I also think he likes to show off that all by himself he can grow chiles in greater quantity and of higher quality than me and my whole team of gardeners.

While this familial history probably has something to do with my current relationship to food (and maybe also my current relationship to Mexico), the real reason I became a cook is that when I was thirteen years old I had desperate needs to fulfill. I needed more Nintendo games and a fresh pair of Reebok Pumps. I didn't have any money and my mother didn't have much, so she helped me get an illegal job at a Shoney's restaurant bussing for cash paid under the table. Later, at the age of fifteen, with my only prior experience being in a restaurant and a new taste for financial freedom, I got my first legal job at a Mexican restaurant called Chico's Tacos in Hendersonville, North Carolina. And this is how I was initiated into the culinary profession.

Chico's was a quick-service counter-style restaurant, but we made everything there, from mixing our own spice blends and salsas to frying our own chips and churros and even making all the beans, beef, and chicken. We did not use lard in the tortillas or refried beans, and all the vegetables were fresh, so we were very popular with people in general but especially the vegetarians, Seventh-day Adventists, and hippies that populated our particular area.

The owner of the business at the time was named Kurt Markel. He was a first-generation immigrant born of German parents and spent the first part of his life as a professor of German and English literature. After retiring from teaching, Kurt got into the restaurant business, first owning and operating a locally famous pizza joint for ten years. He sold that to start Chico's Tacos with hopes of franchising the model. The idea was that our area was lacking in healthy and quick Mexican-inspired food. He took an interest in me and loved to teach, so I learned a lot of different things from him. Along with my school and work schedule, he had me reading books. I learned about politics by reading Bill Moyers and religion through Huston Smith and Joseph Campbell; and Kurt made me read the *Utne Reader* every month and helped me with my German homework. He told me to pursue a career in the arts or literature and to never even consider becoming a chef, because I would wind up toiling away under fluorescent lights in a basement somewhere with a bunch of foul-mouthed drunks. I loved it there and worked there throughout high school until I accidentally wound up in Mexico for three months.

After a particularly busy evening slinging tacos, I came home—spattered with salsa, stinking like sour cream, and with bits of beans matted in my hair—to find my mother hosting a Mexican-themed birthday party in our double-wide trailer for our friend Ray. Mexican-themed at the time for progressive thinking hillbillies (the hillbillies in this instance are my mother and her friends) involved Corona beers, Jose Cuervo gold tequila, any hot mess on a paper plate that could be loosely defined as nachos, and quesadillas (pronounced with an "illa" like "gorilla"). I opted out on the victuals, or more appropriately, vittles, and got drunk instead.

In my exhausted and delirious state, I became convinced that I must be Mexican in my soul and that I needed to return to the motherland. I effectively belabored this point to our friend Ray who happened to own multiple apple orchards, a fruit-packing business, and a truck line. This also meant that he employed a lot of human beings that also happened to be Mexican. He asked me if I really wanted to go to Mexico and I insisted that reuniting me with my country was the only reasonable course of action. He told me to pack a bag and grab my birth certificate, which I managed to do before passing out. The contents of my luggage consisted of some clothes, a slicker, three Carlos Castaneda books, two Jack Kerouac books, a disposable camera, a blank journal, and $300 in cash.

I woke up with my head throbbing in unison to someone pounding on my front door. As I opened the door, I did not immediately remember that I was a Mexican to be reunited with my home country, so I was a bit surprised when the man at the door announced that he was Alejandro and that his boss Ray had told him to come get me so that we could go to Mexico. His truck was running, so I found my packed bag and we left. The truck was a Ford F-150 with a single bench seat. Alejandro was six feet, four inches, and in the cramped cabin with us were his wife, their newborn baby, and their five-year-old son. I believe that being able to travel in this fashion for the three-and-a-half straight days we were driving also proves that I am, in fact, Mexican.

I defected to the bed of the pickup for the last few miles, briefly falling asleep, and I woke up seeing more of the cosmos closer to me than I ever had. Although it was around two o'clock in the morning when we arrived in a remote village in the state of Querétaro, in central Mexico, Alejandro's family all got out of bed to greet us. This included his mother, father, little brothers and sisters, aunts and uncles, and even friends who came from neighboring houses. A cookfire was lit, chiles were ground in the molcajete, and fresh tortillas were made by all the daughters in the family. Corn, beans, and chiles in combination is the basis of the Mesoamerican diet. It was slightly exotic but very familiar to me at the same time. When I was growing up in Appalachia, my great-grandmother would make pinto beans, cornbread, Vidalia onions, and pepper vinegar four to five times a week. This was one of my first culinary epiphanies in Mexico.

Shortly after arriving, Alejandro disappeared and I did not see him again for about six weeks. Even if I had wanted to leave there was no clear path as to how, so I just rolled with it. The small village had no running water, no electricity, no telephones, and no police or postal service, so contact with the rest of the world was not an option. The closest town with any of these amenities was an hour's drive down the mountain. The men of the village would leave in the morning to work masonry jobs, herd goats, and work cattle. I would hang out with the women and children and try to be useful collecting firewood, picking chiles, feeding the livestock, or whatever I could do. I spent a lot of time in the kitchen either eating or watching. I was not allowed to cook or prepare anything because I was a man. Once while the mama was gone, the daughters attempted to teach me how to make tortillas. This was a total failure—they were laughing so hysterically that one of them peed her pants.

I would walk around the village every day and I was always invited in by someone because I was a curiosity for a lot of the people: Most of them had never seen a gringo before. Although I had picked up some survival Spanish, I barely understood what was being said, but the older people and children still loved to talk to me for hours. Sometimes it felt like we were having beans for breakfast, lunch, and dinner. I never grew tired of this and the simple, traditional meal of beans, chiles, and tortillas is still my favorite.

Occasionally the matriarch of the family would break up the bean routine. The first time she did this it startled me because I was not sure what was happening. She set a bucket of scalding water by the kitchen door and then nonchalantly walked out to the yard, snatched a chicken by the head, and whipped it around snapping the bird's neck. She dropped it in the scalding bucket and then a herd of children ran over and started plucking the bird. Later that day we had bowls of chicken soup with finely diced onions and jalapeños, fresh tortillas, and a squeeze of lime.

So much of my time spent in Mexico was centered around food that mealtimes became a sort of clock. As you were collecting firewood, you could smell the cookfires of other households being stoked. You knew it was time to make your way to the table when the smell of fresh corn tortillas toasting on a comal started wafting through the air. On an almost weekly basis, I still make the two dishes I have previously described, mainly at home, to help me return to the place that inspired me so much and was the beginning of me seriously considering cooking as a lifetime enterprise.

I thought we were going for a week or two, but I wound up being in Mexico for nearly three months. I gave the camera and journal away to the two oldest daughters in the family. I never took a single picture or wrote anything down. I felt like the beauty of the colors, the smells, and the sounds had left such an indelible memory that I would only betray them with 35 mm disposable camera photos. I did bring back a molcajete for salsa, a blue enamelware pot for beans and chicken soup, and a giant jar of pickled pequín chiles to try and re-create the humble but inspiring food whenever I got homesick for the motherland.

I finally made it back home to my hysterical mother (I had neglected to call her during my sabbatical) sunburned, with the first signs of hair on

my chin, and penniless, except for a few pesos. My job at Chico's was understandably no longer available after failing to call or show up for three months. Kurt had also put the restaurant up for sale and I had decided to get more experience in progressively better places for enrichment, experience, and earnings. I worked multiple restaurant jobs day and night for the next year. I was a waiter at an Irish pub, the meat man at a Jewish deli, and a line cook at an interstate motel all at the same time. I have never liked smoking the weed, but I might have sold a little bit of that, too.

My best friend Rob Ramirez, who I had grown up with, was finishing his first year at North Carolina School of the Arts in Winston-Salem, and we were planning a cross-country trek the first month of summer. We bought backpacks and a thirty-day pass on Greyhound bus lines, and I packed the remaining six books in my Carlos Castaneda series. We traveled from Asheville, North Carolina, to San Francisco and back in those thirty days. There was high adventure for us, but not many culinary epiphanies. We did spend the first ten days in Houston and then Waco, Texas. I believe that I subconsciously started falling in love with Texas at this time. One part of our trip that always stands out in my mind is when some bright lights in an otherwise dark and desolate West Texas woke us. It was 2 a.m. and the bus driver came over the intercom and said,

> "*Buenos dias*, Greyhound passengers. My name is Juan
> and I am your driver. Welcome to El Paso."

This was my first stateside border checkpoint and we were being loaded off and searched. Rob was thoroughly annoyed. But I was excited. I thought maybe I would be kidnapped and taken to Mexico. At the time I could never have imagined that I would one day become a permanent resident, calling the Chihuahuan Desert home.

It was during the last five days of our trip, as Rob and I were making our way home, road weary, nearly broke, and subsisting on cans of franks and beans and bottled water, that I had a realization. He was making plans to go back to school and I was returning to not much of anything. This trip galvanized my resolve to learn how to cook as a profession.

I had made no headway in my lofty dreams of being a painter, writer, or classical guitarist. If I in fact wanted to pursue any of these careers seriously, it occurred to me that I should learn a trade so that I could make money to finance my higher callings. Having only worked in hotels and restaurants, it seemed wise for me to go to culinary school, and it just so happened my town was the home of one of the greatest hotel-restaurant and culinary schools in the nation, Asheville-Buncombe Technical Community College.

This is not a joke. I received an extraordinary education and it was very challenging. In our culinary program, we started with a class of seventy human beings and due to the quality, rigor, and demands of the program, two years later only seven of us graduated. As is the case for most young culinarians attending school in the Americas, we were required to do a three-month internship/externship between years one and two. Not wanting to spend this time too close to home and being baffled by how the logistics of the world works, as I still sometimes am, I was not quite sure what to do. Long before turning age twenty-one allowed me legal entrance to bars, it was the libraries and bookstores that offered sanctuary and solace. It was in one of these locales that I found a *Wine Spectator*—with the talented, smug-faced, and now-deceased chef Charlie Trotter on the cover—announcing their version of the best restaurants in the United States. I came across one place that particularly caught my attention and cross-referenced the place in every book about the industry I could find, which at the time were *Becoming a Chef* and *Culinary Artistry,* both by Dornenburg and Page. The place in question was The Inn at Little Washington.

At the time three of the hottest restaurants in America were The French Laundry in Yountville, California; Charlie Trotter's in Chicago; and The Inn at Little Washington in Virginia. I was mystified by what set these places so distinctly apart from the pack and desperately wanted to bear witness so that I could just hopefully glean a basic understanding of what made them so special. I had not been to very many restaurants at all, much less one that even approached this level of refinement. Stymied by youth, ignorance, and poverty, I could not wrap my head around how I would ever be able to get to the farther places to do the necessary tryout for externship. The Inn at Little Washington was an eight-hour drive north following my Blue Ridge Mountains the whole way. I wanted to understand what the (alien to me) accolades meant. Five Stars, Five Diamonds, Relais & Châteaux? Asking an older schoolmate only elicited, "It means they are the best."

The thing that caught my attention most of all though was the description of the food. *Refined Southern Cuisine with a Touch of Whimsy.* I have always identified with being Southern in a very strong way, but much of my youth was soaked in shame about my surroundings and the food we ate. I had to figure out how the hillbillies could find not just refinement, but redemption through cuisine.

So I spent my entire spring break sitting by the rotary dial phone at the house my roommates and I rented, waiting for a call back from the human resources department of the Inn at Little Washington. My school had told me that I would never get in and that I should explore elsewhere. When The Inn called back, they said I had to do a six-month internship, rather than the three months required and expected by my school. Not wanting to turn down the opportunity, I somehow negotiated a deal to do my six-month internship at the Inn and then come back and do two semesters of school in one semester's time, while working full time to pay for school. I strangely comforted myself in times of doubt with the hillbilly rationale that the only way to train for the Appalachian Trail is to hike the Appalachian Trail.

When I arrived at the Inn, I was given a skullcap, Dalmation pants, and a utility shirt—the uniform for dishwashers. The other externs already had black chef jackets with their names embroidered on them. I surmised this must be an earned garment, so I kept my mouth shut and worked like a fool. I was one of two humans washing all the dishes, pots, pans, and utensils for up to thirty-four chefs, who prepared to serve multicourse menus all night for up to 220 guests, while serving at least eighteen hotel guests afternoon tea and room service, plus going in to all the kitchenware, plates, cutlery, and glasses for a grand finale and then taking out the trash and mopping the kitchen twice. This proved to test the limits of endurance for even the most passionate and enduring youngster. The chefs de partie used to growl at me for smiling and laughing all the time, but I was just so happy to be there. I tried to go as fast as possible to help them prep, but being busy myself I had to learn mostly by observing.

After sixteen weeks in the dish pit, I had a realization that I would be unable to fulfill my assignment from school if I didn't get some more varied experience. I was deathly scared to approach my sous chef but I had to and did. Although all the externs had a cycle in the dish pit, the restaurant had mistakenly labeled me through human resources as a dishwasher. I was told to put on a jacket, but since everyone's was embroidered with their name I didn't have one. My executive sous chef told me to wear his. I spent the remaining eight weeks wearing his jacket, so everyone would mockingly call me Chef. I was then on a high-speed rotation of working the a.m. shift prepping; receiving produce; always cleaning and polishing all the brass, copper, and Jerusalem tile in the kitchen; baking and working pastry from midnight to noon; and even working the front of the house polishing glasses and silver for twelve-hour stretches.

After graduating from culinary school, I went straight back to the Inn at Little Washington. The looming Blue Ridge Mountains were auspicious enough for me. I was enamored of the place. I knew that I would be working past the brink of exhaustion at least six days a week and learning and seeing things that I never knew existed.

It is thrilling to be in the maelstrom of someone else's vision when you submit to the understanding that they know a whole hell of a lot more than you and might need a hand in there. I worked just about every station in the restaurant over the course of four years, and three months before my twenty-fifth birthday, I was offered the job title of Executive Sous Chef. Every house uses a slightly different nomenclature deriving from the brigade system, but in ours I realized again my great fortune of comprehension and understood that my role, along with my limited understanding of the world, was to drive the ship in absence of my captain, and if I were to drop dead, roll me over and carry on. My chef, Patrick O'Connell, who founded the Inn in 1978, called it my lesson in forced maturity. It was eight years total, but my experience at the Inn comprised my entrance into adulthood.

It was shortly after this that I found myself in Texas. During my first and second years in Marfa, I had started doing catering jobs here and there more for fun than for profit. I had grossly underestimated how much I would miss cooking and I wound up making friends with and developing a small client base of lovely humans that allowed me to do just about whatever I was interested in making, as long as there was food. Some examples that come to mind are a yakitori-themed birthday party for seven-year-olds, a family-style Ethiopian dinner for a Mexican art opening, and a vegan/ Indian/Texas BBQ for two gents getting married. I learned also from the wave of landed gentry that preceded me that it is part of your civic duty

as a Marfa resident to do something that the community needs. My only other skill set is being loud and obnoxious, so it was time to get cooking and feed the humans.

There are compromises to be made when you commit to serving your community. I initially had no interest in opening my own restaurant. I was still convalescing after spending the majority of my life working in other people's restaurants. But, from the moment my boots hit the ground in Marfa, I spent every day being accosted and harangued by my fellow citizens who all had the same basic question:

"When are you going to open a restaurant?"

I had no courage or capital, only compunction.

After a successful and sometimes challenging run with a restaurant that my buddy/business partner and I called Miniature Rooster, I decided to close the business as a restaurant and to continue to do catering events. I was a little nervous about how I was going to survive in this situation, but the chain of events turned out to be quite the blessing in disguise.

There seemed to be an event every week in Marfa and the Capri, which at the time was functioning as an event space, had newfound popularity as a destination location for weddings. I was cooking for all of those and at the same time doing community dinners and artists' dinners for Ballroom Marfa. I was doing private dinners and parties in people's homes in Marfa and traveling to New York or Los Angeles to do private dinners or parties for people that I had met in Marfa.

I had met Virginia Lebermann when I first moved to Marfa, but it was around this time that she and I were talking at a party. We had talked a few times before about putting a functional kitchen in the Capri, to raise the level of quality of the events. She said,

"Sweetie, we need to take this Capri deal up a few notches.
We need a proper kitchen and a bar and I want it to be
like nothing else anyone has ever seen and it has to be *sessy*!"

Right around this time we had started dating, too.

We decided to go meet her longtime (and my newfound) friend Sean Daly—actor, artist, set designer, and ambidextrous life liver extraordin-aire—at our favorite lunch spot, Il Buco in New York City, and pitch him the project of helping us design and build out the space. He must have said yes, because after a long, boozy lunch we somehow woke up in the tiny and oh so lovely Hotel Budir in Iceland. It was the middle of March and I think our rationale was that we would be able to hole up somewhere beautiful, see the Northern Lights, and draw up the master plan for the Capri. A white-out blizzard came in and we were stuck for three days in the tiny hotel. We never saw the Northern Lights, but we sat by the fire as the only guests at the Hotel Budir sipping my favorite schnapps *brennivín* (also affectionately called Black Death), eating cod liver and rotten shark, and armed with our notebooks and Sean Daly's crayon collection. This is the time that I consider the Capri to have been born.

Cocktails

In Oaxaca, when you arrive at someone's home, they offer a small and delicate copita of mezcal. When you arrive at the Capri, we offer you an inappropriately large mezcal.

Ruger .45

THIS IS OUR RIFF ON the French 75. It is named after an old friend, Charles Ruger. When Virginia called to ask his permission to name a cocktail after him we were worried this particular concoction was not a reflection of his usual vodka, soda, lime preference. He responded, "Oh, Virginia, every cocktail has something to do with me." We emphasized our regional ingredients in this drink by adding prickly pear wine to the basic gin French 75. We make our own prickly pear wine when the season is right, and just as with grape-based wine, you can end up with different flavor profiles. The one we prefer for the Ruger .45 we have called Tropical. Prickly pear wine has become steadily more available commercially, but you can also use prickly pear juice or prickly pear concentrate, both available online or in specialty stores.

Serves 1

1 oz (30 ml)	dry gin
1½ oz (45 ml)	Prickly Pear Wine (page 228), prickly pear juice, or prickly pear concentrate
¼ oz (7 ml)	fresh lime juice
¾ oz (20 ml)	simple syrup (1:1 ratio of sugar to water)
3 oz (90 ml)	Prosecco or other dry sparkling wine
	Fall aster flower, for garnish (optional)

Combine the gin, prickly pear wine, lime juice, and simple syrup in a mixing glass filled with ice. Stir until chilled, about 45 rotations. Strain into a chilled coupe glass and top with Prosecco. Garnish with a fall aster flower or nothing at all.

Conquistador

THE RUM WE USE IN this drink comes from Guatemala. Rum is distilled from sugarcane. As with other warmer regions in the Caribbean and Latin America where sugarcane is grown, this distilled spirit is a commodity that was historically produced by indigenous populations for Europeans and for export to Europe. Therefore, we call it the Conquistador.

Serves 1

1	egg white
¾ oz (20 ml)	agave syrup
1 oz (30 ml)	fresh orange juice
½ oz (15 ml)	heavy (whipping) cream
2 oz (60 ml)	Ron Zacapa 23 Sistema Gran Reserva rum
	Expressed orange twist or hummingbird bush flower (optional, and only when in season), for garnish

Combine the egg white, agave, orange juice, cream, and rum in a cocktail shaker. Dry shake vigorously. Add ice and shake again. Double-strain into a coupe glass and garnish with an expressed orange twist or hummingbird bush flower.

Mexican in Paris

LONG BEFORE WE OPENED THE Capri, Virginia and I entertained all the passersby in Marfa at our house. One particular week we had given a number of cocktail parties, and our home bar was somewhat depleted. One of these evenings a friend of ours, Jonathan Mergele, resorted to pouring tequila into his glass of champagne. In justification he said, with a wink, "We'll just call this one a Mexican in Paris." Desperate times require desperate measures! When we opened the restaurant, we gussied up Jonathan's creation to be fit for the menu, while still honoring its origins.

Serves 1

2 oz (60 ml)   reposado tequila

1–3 dashes   lime bitters

Champagne, preferably Moët

Expressed lime twist, for garnish

Combine the tequila and bitters in a cocktail shaker filled with ice and shake vigorously for a few seconds. Double-strain, to remove any tiny shards of ice, into a coupe glass. Top with Champagne. Garnish with an expressed lime twist.

Oaxacan Old-Fashioned

THIS PRECIOUS LIBATION COMES FROM the renowned cocktail bar Death & Co in New York's East Village. We put it on our menu because of our affinity for Oaxaca and it became an instant hit. We like to give credit where all credit is due.

Serves 1

	Bar spoonful of agave nectar
5 dashes	mole bitters
½ oz (15 ml)	reposado tequila
1½ oz (45 ml)	mezcal
	Raw cacao bean, for garnish
	Orange twist, for garnish

Combine the agave, bitters, tequila, and mezcal in a mixing glass filled with ice. Stir until chilled, about 40 rotations. Strain into a double rocks glass over a single large ice cube. Shave the raw cacao bean over the drink and garnish with an orange twist.

Shane Delaney

THIS IS THE FAVORED CONCOCTION of our friend and Capri designer Sean Daly, so we cheekily named it after his alter ego. Sean has a constantly evolving roster of nicknames for his friends, so Rocky started calling him Shane Delaney one day. Pickled okra and tequila are a wild combination and a perfect reflection of the blending of cultures in this region.

Serves 1

2 oz (60 ml)	blanco tequila, preferably Fortaleza
1½ oz (45 ml)	pickled okra juice
2	pickled okra, for garnish

Combine the tequila and pickle juice in a mixing glass filled with ice. Stir until chilled, about 36 rotations. Strain into a double rocks glass over cracked ice. Garnish with 2 pickled okra on a skewer.

The Germaine

OUR HEAD BARTENDER, JERRAM, PRESENTED this cocktail one day as a new option for the menu. We liked it so much it went straight on the list that night. Rocky's nickname for Jerram is Germaine. It will forever stay on the menu in Jerram's honor, because we had been naming drinks after our friends and special people in our lives and it was time that he had his.

Serves 1

¾ oz (20 ml)	agave syrup
¾ oz (20 ml)	fresh lime juice
1 oz (30 ml)	fresh orange juice
½ oz (15 ml)	añejo rum, preferably Ron Abuelo 7 años
1½ oz (45 ml)	bourbon
	Orange wedge and rosemary sprigs, for garnish

Combine the agave, lime juice, orange juice, rum, and bourbon in a cocktail shaker. Shake vigorously for 10 seconds. Strain into a rocks glass over crushed ice. Garnish with an orange wedge and a sprig of rosemary. Lightly touch the rosemary with a lit kitchen torch to make it smolder.

Hibiscus Margarita

THE CONCEPT AND THE INGREDIENTS of this drink are straight from Mexico. We call it a "good for you" margarita because of all the vitamins in the dried hibiscus flowers. We have expanded a bit on the simpler traditional drink, which is generally shaken with fresh lime juice and some sort of sweetener, by muddling the fruit for extra flavor. It is by far the most popular drink on our menu.

Serves 1

1 cup (120 g)	dried hibiscus flowers
2 cups (475 ml)	boiling water
1 oz (30 ml)	agave syrup
3	lime wedges, plus 1 wedge for garnish
2	lemon wedges
1	orange wedge
2 oz (60 ml)	reposado tequila
	Mint springs, for garnish

In a heatproof bowl, combine the hibiscus flowers with the boiling water and let steep for 10 minutes. Strain, pressing the flowers to extract all of the juice, then let cool to room temperature. Combine 1 ounce (30 ml) of the cooled tea, the agave syrup, and citrus wedges in a cocktail shaker and muddle gently. Add the tequila and fill the shaker with ice. Shake vigorously for about 5 seconds. Strain into a chilled margarita glass. Garnish with a lime wedge and several mint sprigs.

Kissing Bandit

THERE ARE JUST SOME DRINKS that immediately make you feel you might accidentally kiss someone that you probably shouldn't. This is one of them, hence the name.

COCKTAIL
Serves 1

¾ oz (20 ml)	fresh lemon juice
¾ oz (20 ml)	simple syrup (1:1 ratio of sugar to water)
2 oz (60 ml)	Sage-Infused Sotol (recipe follows)
	Bundle of canyon sage or sage, for garnish

Combine the lemon juice, simple syrup, and sotol in a cocktail shaker filled with ice and shake for 6 seconds. To remove ice shards, double-strain into a tulip or margarita glass. Garnish with sage bundle.

SAGE-INFUSED SOTOL
Makes 750 ml

1 bottle (750 ml)	sotol reposado, preferably Hacienda de Chihuahua
12–15	fresh sage leaves

Pour the sotol (reserving the bottle) into a nonreactive container. Add the sage leaves and let sit at room temperature for about 8 hours. Strain through cheesecloth and return the mixture to the empty bottle. Infused sotol will keep indefinitely.

Spicy Chihuahua

MARGARITAS SPIKED WITH A LITTLE jalapeño seem to be ubiquitous these days. We wanted to make our own version of a spicy cocktail. Although the ingredients that we use are more Oaxacan, we put a different twist on it and make it in Marfa, which is in the Chihuahuan Desert, hence the Spicy Chihuahua.

Serves 1

1 oz (30 ml)	fresh lime juice
2 oz (60 ml)	mezcal, preferably Del Maguey Vida
1 oz (30 ml)	Spicy Agave (recipe follows)
	Sal de Chihuahua, for rimming (recipe follows)
	Jalapeño, for garnish

Combine the lime juice, mezcal, and agave in a cocktail shaker and shake vigorously. Rim a double rocks glass with Sal de Chihuahua and strain the drink into the rimmed glass. Garnish with a jalapeño.

SAL DE CHIHUAHUA
Serves 1

1 part	Sal de Chapulín (page 202) or sal de gusano
1 part	chicatana and cardamom sea salt
2 parts	gochugaru (Korean red chili flakes)

Mix all the ingredients on a small plate.

SPICY AGAVE
Makes 4 cups (950 ml)

10	serrano peppers, seeded and chopped
2 cups (475 ml)	agave syrup

In a small pot, combine the serranos, agave syrup, and 2 cups (475 ml) water and bring to a boil over high heat. Remove from the heat and let cool. Strain the spicy agave and transfer to an airtight glass or plastic container. Keep refrigerated.

The Capri Hot Chocolate

IN HER EARLY TWENTIES, VIRGINIA had the pleasure of going with a friend to Tosca in San Francisco for a drink. This was long before its new iteration under April Bloomfield's command. The red booths were held together by duct tape and the jukebox really only had Italian opera on it. In other words, it was perfect. Their house drink, lined up on the bar, was hot chocolate with Cognac. It was a mind-blowing discovery for a girl from rural Texas, one we wanted to replicate for our guests at the Capri. We make ours with tequila because no one knows what Cognac is down here in Southwest Texas. You'll see how long this batch lasts, depending on the weather, and your guests' appetite for hot chocolate spiked with booze.

Serves 6–8

2 qt (2 liters)	organic whole milk
2 heaping cups (400 g)	chocolate pistoles
2 disks (4 oz)	Mexican chocolate, roughly chopped
2 oz (60 ml)	tequila, mezcal, or brandy per person, for serving
	Whipped cream, cinnamon stick, and marshmallows (optional), for garnish

In a saucepan, bring the milk to a slow simmer over medium-high heat. Add the chocolate and whisk until melted. Strain the hot chocolate through a chinois or fine-mesh sieve and keep warm. To make 1 drink, fill a cup or mug three-quarters full with cocoa. Add the liquor of choice or serve on the side in a separate cup. Serve with fresh whipped cream, a cinnamon stick, and marshmallows if you like (though the most important part is the copita of tequila, mezcal, or brandy that you add).

The Birth of the Capri

We wanted the Capri to embody the feeling of the history on the border. We wanted the air to feel thick with possibility and the thrill of cultural abandon.

THE BIRTH OF THE CAPRI

by Virginia

The Capri is inextricably tied to the town of Marfa and its surroundings. It is an integral piece of a whole community rather than an independent business or restaurant. The adobe building itself is constructed from the local dirt of Marfa. This particular space with its fundamental nature and character could not exist anywhere else. The land, sky, flora, fauna, and people, the cultural realities of the region itself, all articulate in conjunction to define the unique character of the Capri. It is our role to provide sustenance, but not only through food. Through art, music, cultural explorations, and a multiplicity of textures, we explore all of the senses at the Capri. It is a roadside saloon purely by dint of the fact that it sits on Highway 90, which rolls through town heading west toward Valentine, Texas, and east toward Alpine, Texas. The Capri sits in Marfa proper but not on the main drag. It is four blocks off the beaten path. Some people never come across it and never know it is there. Again, it is in Marfa, where high art resides on the high desert plains, a town populated by some who have never lived anywhere else, and some who have never traveled to anywhere else, and is visited by people who drive in and fly in from all over the globe. People from every kind of life—every decision, every nondecision, every circumstance—walk through our doors. I have seen the dining room filled with an entire motorcycle club of Bandidos from El Paso. I have seen it filled by the board of the Museum of Modern Art. Most guests are shocked by the glamorous oasis they have entered just off the highway. It is elevated in design, but just a little. It is respectful of its origins.

People say the Capri feels like home, like sitting on the floor for dinner in the library at my house, where we used to host artists before we opened the restaurant. There is a good chance I'll get to meet you or see you when you are there. But there is a good chance I might shock you because I'm running around in a black silk dress, barefoot. It is a restaurant but has a very small and particular menu. Rocky struggles to consistently offer vegan options, though his dream as a young man was to have the first Michelin-starred vegan restaurant. We are a mess living in a famous little outpost. Even though we are a mess, it's likely you will have fun here. At the very least, you won't go hungry.

The Capri is constantly uplifted by a community of individuals who bring their expertise to the layers of details that create the whole of the experience at the restaurant. They are the characters that comprise the always-unfolding narrative of the Capri. They are our co-conspirators, our family. They are the ones who lend their support, take issue when it needs to be taken, and listen to us rattle on endlessly about things we don't understand. These people put meat on the bones of every endeavor we might undertake. They share their ideas, resources, and hard work to imagine and realize the reality of the Capri. We all come together through thick and thin to give this beautiful property its soul, and to create a place for human gathering of which we can be proud. I have an unwavering respect and admiration for these people.

I purchased the Capri and its sister property, the Thunderbird Motel, in 2004. The building that houses the Capri was originally a World War II army airfield hangar. Marfa was the site of military installations from 1911 to 1946. During World War II, it was used as an outpost to guard the US-Mexican border. In the 1940s, the airfield in Marfa was closed and the hangars sold off and moved to town by their new owners. To my knowledge, there are just three of these repurposed adobe and steel hangars in Marfa: The Capri, and two on The Block, the Judd Foundation property. The Capri building was rebuilt by the Pierce family, Marfa locals who also owned the Thunderbird Motel across the street. They covered over the old adobe structure of the motel with the fabulous pink diamonds made from plywood that were in vogue at the time and remain characteristic of certain 1960s roadside motels—pure Americana. The Thunderbird Motel was built in the 1950s and soon after its owners opened a diner as well, called the Thunderbird Restaurant. I'm told that was where everyone met for coffee, breakfast, and lunch. Although the pink diamonds on the building no longer exist, the old Thunderbird Restaurant sign in its original state is still outside the Capri. Somewhere, I think we still have the old velvet matador paintings that peppered the walls of the original Thunderbird diner.

When we first acquired the Capri, we reopened it not as a restaurant, but as a cultural arts project aligned with Ballroom Marfa, the art space that Fairfax Dorn and I had started together a few years before. The inaugural event was held in October 2007, when Sonic Youth played in what was still a construction site. The concert was a collaboration between Ballroom and Donald Judd's Chinati Foundation for one of their annual Open House Weekends. Although we had already transformed the Thunderbird back into a functioning motel, I honestly was not quite sure what the Capri would become. There were two thousand people in attendance at the Sonic Youth concert, filling the interiors and the gardens and hanging from the scaffolding. It was terrifying to witness the mayhem, yet it also gave me a sense that this space could be utterly versatile. It could be filled with musicians, artists, and revelry, but by design it would possess the warmth to host intimate gatherings, or perhaps one day a restaurant and bar. Just after that initial event, we finished all the basic construction on the building and planted extensive native gardens over what had previously been a blacktop parking lot. I then let the building lie fallow and the gardens grow and mature for eight years. Every now and then people would rent the barren space to have events. I wasn't sure what to do with it. Until Rocky arrived.

Rocky Barnette had landed in Marfa a few years before, in 2008, and had immediately became a mainstay of our lives through Ballroom. For each art opening at Ballroom we hosted a community dinner in the barebones, pre-restaurant Capri. He would cater and orchestrate these dinners for three hundred to four hundred people. Before Rocky's appearance in Marfa, Vance Knowles, our founding and beloved music director at Ballroom, used to call Fairfax and me to let us know of unexpected guests coming to dinner.

> "Ladies, I mean, Ballroom Catering, it seems we
> have twenty-two people for dinner tonight instead
> of the expected eight."

Vance does not cook. I'm still not sure to this day if he knows how to cook an egg. Fairfax and I would rise from our Ballroom desks, run to her house, and start frantically chopping onions. We did everything. There was no one else to call for help.

By far, one of my favorite memories of pre-Capri Rocky cooking was an Ethiopian dinner he cooked for a Ballroom group show called *In Lieu of Unity*, consisting solely of artists from Mexico. We didn't have enough utensils in the whole town to serve over four hundred people. So Rocky ingeniously devised a plan to serve Ethiopian cuisine, which requires no flatware, only injera, the Ethiopian flatbread used as both sustenance and utensil. All the guests were mystified by the whimsical juxtaposition of Ethiopian food for a group show of Mexican artists. Through the years Rocky and the Ballroom team continued to work together to create dinners of all shapes and sizes for visitors, who often felt concern and sometimes panic over the lack of culinary options in Marfa. Eventually it all came together. We had a classically trained chef on the loose in the culinarily challenged town of Marfa. We had a town with a lack of great restaurants and an incredible adobe structure sitting empty without its next story unfolding inside. We had a match made in heaven.

The idea to open the restaurant happened on a trip from New York back to Marfa. Rocky and I had been spending most of our time in New York for a year or so and I was ready to recalibrate the majority of time back to Marfa. I was always intrigued with the idea of incorporating the culinary arts into the broader spectrum of art and cultural studies at Ballroom. Rocky and I felt his passion for Mexican culture and the indigenous people of the Chihuahuan Desert would ignite an exciting concept for a new restaurant in Marfa, while simultaneously connecting the Capri back to the Ballroom as an extension of this well-established cultural foundation.

Although it certainly happens elsewhere in the world, the idea of connecting food to the region and cultures of the past had not yet been explored in a formal, elevated context in Marfa. We felt the idea of connecting both food and design to the regional past as well as the present would create a unique research and development project that would require travel, resource materials, high adventure, and far-flung ideas.

Once we determined to move the project forward and transform the Capri into an operational restaurant, we called our friend Sean Daly from the road—driving either in or out of Marfa, I can't remember which, as it always seemed we were going one way or the other. We knew we would need all of Sean's mysterious talent for design and storytelling in order to create the perfect environment. We told him about creating a place where we wanted to have a drink in Marfa. We told him a tale of Texas history and a touch of madness. He didn't hesitate. He was on board for the design project. He knowingly responded,

"Welcome, we've been expecting you."

He already understood the essence of the project. His words are now forever memorialized on the matchbooks at the Capri.

Sean's background is in set design, which I believe fosters his mercurial sense of design development. He is forever creating new environments for movies or advertising campaigns. He is not tied to one specific era of design, certain furniture designers, or styles. He is not repetitious in his use of materials or solutions to design questions. He is dedicated to the idea that each new backdrop tells its own unique story. His process was a long and wandering path to a perfect solution for a space and concept as unique as the Capri, part restaurant, part cultural laboratory, and part-time music venue.

The Capri interior was a barren space when we decided to open the restaurant and participate in the unfolding culinary world of Marfa. We had an open palette to work with. In its state at the time there were only exposed adobe walls, concrete floors, and a longleaf pine ceiling. The architectural firm Lake|Flato from San Antonio had designed the initial creation of spaces and proportions around 2004. Now, years later, we had the opportunity to bring the building alive with the details of atmosphere, interior design, and a story.

As we embarked on the next phase of design to create life in the space, I thought about the old mercantile store I had grown up close to, just down the ranch road. The rural mercantile stores were gathering places for ranchers, farmers, and their families. People collected there for a simple lunch, usually consisting of one option on the menu, while others came to purchase basic supplies from the shelves stocked with cans of coffee, shortening, flour, sugar, and beans. There was usually a broom or two to be had and a stack of twine if you needed to tie some things together. But the experience was mostly social. They were the places to find your friends, sit at a table with a cigarette and a soda, and catch up on the gossip and tribulations of your neighbors. It was also where you went

to talk a lot about the weather. Additionally, I thought about the famous old bars on the Texas-Mexico border. The Cadillac Bar in Nuevo Laredo and the Kentucky Club in Juárez have always held a nostalgic little corner of my brain. In their heyday, they were fabulously dark and wild and a little bit naughty and all the barmen were impeccably dressed in white jackets and bow ties. It seems to me that that is what life should always feel like—just a little too dark, a little too wild, and a little bit naughty. I wanted the Capri to embody the feeling of this history on the border. I wanted the air to feel thick with possibility and the thrill of cultural abandon that these historic bars possessed due to the confluence of North American and Mexican style and spirit.

We executed these dreams and historical musings by employing a few design choices that reflected the past, but were installed with a modern touch. We filled the entire west wall with thirty-six feet of mahogany bar to reflect the enormous old bars on the border that had room for six or more bartenders behind them. The interior doorways are thick with heavy velvet curtains in moss greens and earthy pinks, instead of the red velvet that would have been used in the bars and brothels of the border. We traveled extensively in Mexico to collect the wooden utensils and ceramic pots that fill the expansive shelves behind the bar and rise up to the twenty-foot ceilings. Intermittently, these shelves also house family heirlooms of silver vessels, sculptures, and artwork. The dining tables are antique Indian wedding tables we found at an import store in El Paso. They are worn and patinated by time and reflect the spirit of saloon tables of the past. There is a magic that barstools can create when they are lined up perfectly and make a sculptural statement. They represent the possibility of conversation and a loss of heavy inhibition. Our barstools are brass and quite modern with sleek lines, but they are brought back to the past by the easy green leather seats. Together these elements create a mise-en-scène reminiscent of a more lavish approach to design that conjures the past. It is intended to be a slight visual relief from the pared-down modern design elements for which Marfa is now so famous.

During the design process we had to make some unusual choices in creating spaces within a somewhat vast hangar. To create spatial fluidity in what is a perfect rectangular box, we decided to build the prep kitchen as a separate building connected to the main building only by a shade structure. The main building houses the plating room, main dining room

and bar, and a smaller room off the dining room and bar we have always called the Tea Room. I had dreams of serving proper fantastical Old World high tea in there, but for now we have a piano. The Capri is surrounded by a native botanical garden boasting over four hundred native species from the American Southwest and Northern Mexico. It was originally designed by the brilliant landscape architect Christy Ten Eyck. The gardens wrap around the entire periphery of the building, lending life and movement to an otherwise fairly austere plastered adobe structure. I relish the moments watching people soak in the abundance. You can bring your drinks out there, eat out there, wander.

Behind the restaurant proper is a large unadorned adobe warehouse space that we open for concerts and events related to the art foundations in town, like Ballroom Marfa and the Chinati Foundation. I can't imagine how many musicians have played in that room. Someone must know, but I don't. The likes of Sonic Youth, Yo La Tengo, Tinariwen (former Tuareg freedom fighters from Mali), Las Alteñas (the all-female mariachi band from San Antonio), Weyes Blood, and William Basinski, to name a few, have played in this hall of music.

The distance between the separate prep kitchen and the dining room in the main building, required, for the servers and kitchen crew, a short skateboard ride down a long sidewalk in the garden. It was a somewhat impractical solution, considering the need to traverse the elements outdoors with food in hand. To solve the problem we created a plating room connected to the restaurant. It was a matter of style over function. This plating room is where all the action happens. The door to this room opens at the south end of the bar. The guests watch the intensity and artistry as they walk past or stop to take a photograph. The plating room is where Rocky executes the final touches and plates dishes before they are swept away into the dining room. It's high theatrics in there. There are bushels of flowers picked for salads. Billowing smoke rises and falls in plumes from the ceremonial Mayan white copal incense always burning on the altar in the plating room. The Mayans saw visions in the smoke of the copal; I think Rocky does, too. There is an altar in this room that is curated every day before service and broken down each night. It consists of Maurice, a brass monkey; San Pascual, the patron saint of cooking; Santa Muerte, our Lady of holy death; Jesus of the Bleeding Heart; and objects I wouldn't know how to describe. It is the installation of a wild man, slightly unhinged.

There is a dance always occurring in the plating room, the constant and precise motions of knife-wielding people, bubbling liquids, and scorching flames. Artwork on the walls creates a cocoon for the pulsing scene on the floor. One piece is Matthew Day Jackson's video installation *Little Boy and Fat Man* (2009), the models of nuclear bombs constantly dropping from the sky, the perpetual anxiety of imminent disaster. When I chose to move that piece to the plating room it felt realistic and appropriate for that particular space. I also hung two photographs from a 2008 Ballroom show entitled *Hello Meth Lab in the Sun*. The artists are Jonah Freeman, Justin Lowe, and Alexandre Singh. These photographs dig into the idea of alchemy, specifically as it pertains to altering ingredients into drugs and food into electrical charges. On the south wall, Dana Schutz's, *Head of Timothy Leary* (2005) doesn't need much explanation, I don't think. It all flows back to the underlying pulse of a madhouse. On the eastern wall is *Aurora Borealis* by Jem Goulding (2016). The art in this room was a conscious decision to visually separate the inspiration and theatrics of the plating room from the functionality most associate with the kitchen of a restaurant.

If you are a local or someone we admire from a distant land, Rocky will come out of the plating room and announce your arrival in a booming voice while clapping with a warmth that extols the excitement of your arrival. It is our house and you are treated as a guest in our home. In the fall and winter, there is a fire burning in the bar to warm your bones. In the warmer months, the porches and courtyards become the most sought-after spaces in which to linger over cocktails and dinner under the blue skies and infinite stars. When it is high fly season in the desert, we burn copious amounts of copal incense in the gardens to clear the air of pestilence. It is a fluid state of everchanging variables. We have spring winds that blow consistently at forty to eighty knots and whip up dust storms that feel apocalyptic. At almost five thousand feet in elevation, the desert sun can bake your brain if you stand out in it too long. When monsoon season arrives, the rains can be so fierce they seep through the adobe walls and erode the mud bricks. We live in and with the elements at the Capri and they all sneak in and out of the cracks between the mud brick, plaster, and steel.

HOW THE WEST ONCE WAS

by Sean Daly

The first time I passed through Marfa was in 2001, shortly after 9/11. I had driven across Texas for a month of soul searching and was looking for a way to make sense of the newly unwrapped world. Marfa was, and still is, a very small point in a massive space. After a long ride speeding through the vast and open terrain, a little town sprang up out of nowhere like a mirage. When I finally pulled into town, I not only felt but saw that Marfa was indeed different from any other place I had ever been. The evening air was cooler, and smelled like a mix of wet highway, creosote, and wood-burning stoves. Except for the sound of a distant barking dog or a truck on Highway 90 changing gears a mile away, there was a palpable stillness and the silence was deafening. For the first time, I understood how immense the sky was, and I felt dwarfed by the landscape all around.

The next day I witnessed the phenomenon of "optical horizon," something I first learned about in Australia's outback. Due to the altitude and geography of the town, the naked eye is tricked into seeing not one horizontal edge of earth where it meets the sky, but many stacked on top of each other. Seeing these points as they fade into the distance you realize the vastness between horizons, and with the sky-to-earth ratio I'm not sure exactly how far you can see on a clear day, but it's far. This experience was mixed with the never-ending magnificence of the cloud formations overhead. The clouds sometimes contain electrical storms so far away their thunder is not heard. When the storms do come to town, enjoy the show. Before I arrived I had found a vintage postcard from town. It read; "Marfa, How the West Once Was." I understood.

I often feel that I met Virginia in another life. Our first encounter in this life, however, was in 1999, through her cousin, who had invited me to attend a few art-related events in Texas. I later would return to Texas many times, and make the long drive across the state on the back roads, pulling into

faraway juke joints, and seeing the places where Virginia and her cousin had spent time as kids. I came to know Marfa, in particular, more intimately as a guest of Virginia's and Fairfax Dorn's just as they were starting Ballroom in 2003. Along with Vance Knowles, who was programming music at the space, the three would build a vibrant destination for artists, musicians, writers, and filmmakers. Since I had experience as production designer and art director in films, I began working with Ballroom as the chief designer for their fundraising events in New York, Los Angeles, Houston, and Miami.

In the beginning, Virginia, Fairfax, and Vance all wore many hats—curators, booking agents, and most of all, hosts. Frequently after Ballroom gallery openings, the trio would hold open community dinners, cooking for two hundred guests as if it were no problem. Fairfax and Virginia both possess the most exquisite sets of skills when hosting, on any level but here for an entire town. A kitchen drawer at Fairfax's house held silverware for three hundred guests, and a cabinet in Virginia's held hundreds of plates and wineglasses. Both Virginia and Fairfax's homes would often become extensions of the Ballroom's generosity to the community. We would joke about how they had started not only a nonprofit but inadvertently opened a restaurant. But despite their facility, the team would often reach out to the chefs in town and ask for a hand. One of my first meetings with Rocky was on one of these occasions, when he made Cuban barbecue pork for a Ballroom event from a pig called Momma I had once met. (Rest in peace, Momma, you were delicious.)

When Virginia took ownership of the Capri space, it had, for decades, served as a diner and motel. Virginia and the architects of the firm Lake|Flato removed all of the temporary and additional interior walls that had been added over the years, revealing the beautiful cavernous building. Later Virginia and Christy Ten Eyck's design team planted gardens filled with Texas native species. When the space was finished, it was used for weddings and events; the next phase would take a few more years to pull together. Finally, Virginia called me and asked,

"Do you think you could design us a bar in Marfa
where we would want to drink?"

Of course I said yes, and thus began my ongoing collaboration on the design of the Capri.

In my film and photography design work, I try to bring in a collection of objects and textures that give the characters a visual creative reality. The practice of dramaturgy, although it generally applies to stage plays, similarly applies to my work. It is about the construction of aesthetic and dramatic spaces through design and lighting, and building settings that all translate into an emotional experience when viewed by the audience. When trying to describe my job, a journalist tasked with interviewing me came up with the term "character architect." Ultimately, I would use the same process to include many dramatic and intimate touches in the design of the Capri—narrative elements that expanded design into story.

Everything at the Capri is like this. Each design element is reflective of the environment around us, from the branding to the drapery. The calm gray of the concrete in the walls and on the polished floor is the reminder of the heavy summer storm clouds in Marfa that drop all the much-needed rain on the region. The wall behind our bar is built from local adobe bricks, and the dusty browns and yellowy beiges mixed with stands of dried grass and straw, slightly shift in color according to the sun and the weather. In the evening, the adobe takes on a warm glow from the light from the fireplace.

The deep blue of our logo is inspired by the dark blue starry night skies that hang so low over Texas, and the deep-blue waters that surround the restaurant's namesake, the midcentury motor hotel Holiday Capri Inn, which once stood on the property. In the time before chain motels and interstate freeways, the giant neon sign at the motel would have been a welcomed beacon to travelers. All that remains now is the forty-foot shell of the sign. The word "Capri" is no longer visible but the sign still stands and frequently we have guests who come back to see what Marfa looks like today, who are pleased to see what the space has become.

At the start of the Capri buildout, I walked through the raw space, naming the rooms of the restaurant to come: We would have a Tea Room, a Private Dining Room, the Astronomer's Lounge upstairs in the attic. The main room at the Capri is exposed to the gardens through a full walls of windows, so we let the gardens dictate the interior color palette. Studying the plants and rocks outside during the bleak winter months, I discovered a vibrant palette; bright splotches of rusts on the leaves or the almost technicolor turquoise green of the tall leather stools at the bar, inspired by naturally occurring mineral deposits in the local rock called Marfa agate.

In this way the Capri has become an intimate version of the town itself, a community more than just a typical bar or restaurant. We want it to feel familiar, yet magical, as if it is a place from a dream we all share. When guests enter, they usually take a beat and look around. First timers will sometimes seem stunned. Regulars ease back into the space like they've missed it. It feels extravagant, ethereal, yet also like you're arriving home, to family. Walk into the Capri and we will promptly throw a log on the fire, offer a chair, and pour you a drink—all as if to say,

"Welcome, we've been expecting you."

On an early trip to Marfa, I had had a serendipitous experience that set the tone for creating what would eventually become the Capri. I wandered into Livingston's, the old-fashioned ranch supply store. The store is authentic and is still the place for ranchers to order anything they need for their business—a galvanized tub or replacement hose for watering live-stock, or the wire for fencing that stretches out into the horizon. I asked permission to take some pictures.

I pointed the viewfinder toward the floor to get it to focus. On top of the creaky, wide wood boards was written a love letter to local history, told in pieces of linoleum flooring, swatches and samples representing the many decades worth of designs. Here and there were small exposed tacks keeping pieces in place along an overlapping edge. Some of the pieces were large enough for a customer to see the full pattern and its available borders. There were Art Deco lines and Streamline Moderns pushed up next to '40s oversized floral patterns, a Persian carpet paisley glued onto an atomic Space Age or boomerang pattern, all quilted into one. Time and foot traffic had caused certain areas to wear away, but some were patched over in very different colored or patterned pieces. Placement was brilliantly haphazard and random, almost as if created by a collage artist interested in time travel. The Livingston's floor display was a kaleidoscopic map, patterns telling the history of a town survived by drought, world war, population booms, trips to the moon, and on into the future.

I thought of these floors often, and I was inspired to re-create them some-how, maybe as large-scale paintings. It was in this way that the strange beauty of Livingston's floors eventually became Capri's beautiful tapestries, created by a family deep in Mexico. These artisans took my photos and masterfully picked up the discrepancies in colors, including where the actual floors had faded. They found ways to exaggerate the worn faux wood-grain patterns in a '40s linoleum, and included a few tiny strokes to portray the shine of metal staples actually penetrating the floor. One of these pieces now hangs proudly above the main fireplace in the bar, and another is in the Tea Room on the floor under Kathryn the Great, our house piano.

Many of the ideas for the design of the Capri came in this same way—exploring and experiencing Marfa and the surrounding environs, wandering and dreaming. Much of the design also grew from the seeds of ideas planted over the course of my then decade-long friendship with Virginia. Virginia and I began to imagine a group of invented characters, based mostly on the stories of our own grandmothers. We imagined their stories of traveling the world a century ago, experiencing other cultures. How would they translate those experiences into today's times? How would what they witnessed inform their hospitality out here on the far Western part of the New American *frontera*? We wanted to capture this collision of beautiful objects possibly imported from Paris and Rome, with the rough and wild terrain of the Chihuahuan Desert.

On a scouting and sourcing trip in central Mexico, we went looking for the longtime maker of the traditional church candles that Virginia had always burned in her home. We wound up wandering into the amazing world of Charlie Hall, now our good friend. In Charlie's workshops nothing is made by machine, and everything is created in the most authentic and traditional ways, including the candles and hand-blown glassware. Charlie's candles are produced by artists hand-ladling wax down a center wick. The slow process is exacting and the artisans measure to confirm the circumference and length of the candle. We now have an exclusive relationship with Charlie and his factory to produce our own signature black candles that display a Thunderbird, the insignia of Capri's sister property across the street. Each of Charlie's pieces is made by hand and is said to carry the *alma* or soul of the creator when you hold them. Charlie, a Texas native, employs a team of around thirty and now

produces the candles we burn in the candelabra and all the glasses we use at the bar.

The heavy, oversized velvet drapes at the Capri were chosen to soften the space visually, but also to do the job of blocking drafts in the windy and bitter cold desert winters. To have them made, I went to one of the oldest surviving workshops of its kind, in Hollywood. For over seventy-five years, the craftspeople there have been making historical drapery for movies, and the voluminous pieces you see in theaters and on awards shows. When I brought in my measurements, they pulled out pads of paper and made complicated calculations, the width and height ratio dictating the amount of velvet fabric we would need to order. Through their deep knowledge of drapery they were able to turn 400 pounds of double-sided velvet, into soft, rippling, floor-to-ceiling fabric walls in the cavernous interior doorways of the Capri.

Even the height of the long bar was a considered detail, inspired by the height of the counters at Parisian *tabacs*, the places where you stop to lean against the bar for a standing coffee a few times a day, to buy or read a copy of the newspaper, have a quick glass of wine, and maybe smoke a cigarette while you do both. This same 52-inch height is reminiscent of gates or ranch fences you would lean up against when viewing and visiting cattle and livestock. When we built a mockup of the bar, to try standing at it in the space, it felt just right under eighteen-foot ceilings.

The back bar, which is anchored to the massive adobe wall of the structure, feels almost like it's floating in space. Some of the objects featured on its shelves are gifts from friends and artwork by patrons who live and make work in Marfa. Almost everything in the collection is also utilitarian, the shelves acting as our own style of butler's pantry. Glasses and bottles also live here, and objects shelved with consideration as part of the storytelling décor are placed so that at any point they could be pulled into use for service. Refined, century-old Tiffany & Company wine coolers, Lalique crystal vases, and serving trays with horn handles all share space with engraved Revere bowls proclaiming the achievements of Virginia's ancestors. Populating the shelves next to these relics are Weck storage jars containing the dehydrated and preserved blossoms from the Capri summer gardens, and new adobe bricks handmade from the dirt of Marfa.

The creation of the Capri has been a family affair, the result of longstanding friendship and collaboration. One person who cannot be forgotten in telling the story of the Capri is my friend Henry, Virginia's son. I like to constantly remind him that we have been friends since before he was born. During my design phase, Henry helped test the heights of the stools at the bar, telling me,

> "It's important for small people like me to be able
> to sit at the bar for dinner."

Point taken. He gleefully helped unpack the myriad boxes, sometimes larger than himself—mostly so we could build forts out of them, but the assistance was appreciated. On more than one occasion, he shared his innate childhood clarity and helped me make those 50/50 decisions.

Henry's patience with adults is formidable. He has been dragged, mostly willingly, to every corner of the Earth to try new things that we are also trying for the first time. We've eaten bugs, fermented plants, and some of the spiciest chiles known to man. He has sat though more than his share of "Adult-Only" dinner parties, and has held his own every time. In 2017, when Virginia, Rocky, Henry, and I went to experience Rene Redzepi's Noma Mexico decampment, there was a pause in the dinner service when Henry and I sat together alone, wide-eyed and overwhelmed by everything we had eaten. One of the staff came to check on the only child in the dining room and asked if he enjoyed and understood what he was a part of. Henry very kindly explained not only that he was eight years old, but also that he was pretty much the impetus for the four of us at the table being there. The waiter got a kick out of his response. Henry went on to clarify that he and I were partners in a restaurant of our own, in a small Texas border town called Marfa. The waiter looked at me for confirmation. I nodded and picked up my tequila to toast this ability to explain not only himself, but the world he is from.

He takes a lot after his mother.

Smaller Dishes

We appreciate living in a region so austere it makes you giddy and wide-eyed to hold a locally raised vegetable, which someone else grew, and in quantities plentiful enough for our old roadside saloon. They are, indeed, like jewels, and we are acutely aware of how precious they are.

Jenny Laird's Texas Caviar

OUR FRIEND JENNY LAIRD MADE us laugh one day talking about serving Fritos corn chips and caviar with sour cream at Christmas for her family. In Texas terms it makes perfect sense. The idea originally came from Kevin Sharkey, who is Martha Stewart's right-hand man. Jenny is friends with and a neighbor of Martha. We are not trying to name-drop, just trying to be factual in the lineage of this oh-so-fun and wonderful treat. We are very proud to serve it at the Capri on special occasions, alongside our favorite Texas-made BLK EYE brand vodka, which should be kept in the freezer at all times to ensure maximum chill.

Serves 12

17.5 oz (500 g)	best-quality caviar, such as Black Russian Ossetra, Iranian Ossetra, Kaluga, or Royal Transmontanus
12 bags (9.25 oz/262 g each)	Fritos Corn Chips
16 oz (455 g)	full-fat sour cream
1 bottle (750 ml)	chilled vodka (optional), preferably BLK EYE or your favorite
12	ice glasses (optional)

Serve the caviar however you like: in the original tin, in individual tins, or in a caviar service set up on crushed ice. Provide Fritos and sour cream. We like to serve BLK EYE vodka in shot glasses formed from ice alongside.

Oysters with Prickly Pear Mignonette and Seaweed

WE DON'T SERVE A LOT of seafood in the middle of the desert, although our friend Sean Daly likes to remind us, "You know that this used to all be the bottom of the ocean." We make an occasional exception for certain fish, particularly Gulf of Mexico shrimp (prawns), which come from relatively close by, and are sustainable to boot; and these pristine Island Creek oysters, which come from Duxbury, Massachusetts. The seaweed is a small nod to the native seaweed collectors in the Yucatan and the Mexicans who used to collect algae in the *chinampas*, the floating gardens, of Tenochtitlán near Mexico City. They would form the algae into cakes and age them like cheese, then put a little into a tortilla for sustenance. Because this was so nutritionally dense, a little went a long way. The mignonette is made from the juice, wine, and vinegar of our own *tunas* (prickly pears), though you can substitute cider vinegar or red wine vinegar if you can't get your hands on any *tunas*. The mignonette really tastes best after sitting overnight, so plan ahead and make it at least a few hours in advance of when you'll need it.

Serves 4–6

36	Island Creek select oysters, or your favorite East Coast oyster
4 qt (4 liters)	crushed ice, for serving
1 cup (250 g)	Store-bought wakame seaweed salad
4	limes
1 cup (240 ml)	Prickly Pear Mignonette (recipe follows), for serving

Shuck the oysters, detaching the meat from the shell and flipping over for presentation. Fill 6 individual plates (or one large platter) with crushed ice and divide the oysters among them. Scatter wakame seaweed salad over the oysters. Quarter the limes and slice off the pith running down the center of each wedge. Serve the oysters with the mignonette and limes on the side.

PRICKLY PEAR MIGNONETTE
Makes 3 cups (710 ml)

2 cups (475 ml)	prickly pear vinegar (or unpasteurized apple cider vinegar)
1 cup (240 ml)	fresh prickly pear juice
4	shallots, cut into ⅛-inch (3 mm) dice
4 tbsp	black peppercorns, coarsely ground
1 tsp	kosher (flaked) salt

In a 1-quart (1-liter) jar or other airtight container, combine the vinegar, prickly pear juice, ½ cup (120 ml) water, the shallots, ground pepper, and salt. Shake to combine. Use immediately, or store in the refrigerator for up to one week.

Grilled Avocado Guacamole

WHEN I FIRST STARTED COOKING professionally, I had a series of what I half-jokingly call culinary epiphanies. I tasted the most beautiful and ripe avocados for the first time. Around the same time I had my first slab of seared foie gras. I fantasized that one day I would serve seared avocado in place of foie gras at the Michelin-starred vegan restaurant I dreamed of owning. In reality, I wound up grilling the avocados and making guacamole for a very discerning crowd here on the border. But I guess that's why it's called a fantasy. We serve this with *tostones*, fried plantain chips, to mimic chips and guacamole.

Serves 6
FOR THE TOSTONES

	Neutral oil, such as soybean or avocado, for frying
6	green plantains
	Sal de Chapulín (page 202) or sal de gusano

FOR THE GUACAMOLE

½ cup (120 ml)	fresh lime juice
¼ cup (60 ml)	avocado oil
1 tsp	citric acid (optional)
6	firm-ripe Hass avocados, halved and pitted
	Kosher (flaked) salt and freshly ground black pepper
½	medium red onion, cut into ⅛-inch (3 mm) dice
2	large jalapeños, seeded and cut into ⅛-inch (3 mm) dice
½ cup (20 g)	finely chopped cilantro (fresh coriander)
½ tsp	ground cumin
2 tbsp	extra virgin olive oil

MAKE THE TOSTONES:

Pour at least 4 inches (10 cm) oil into a deep-fryer or other heavy pot. Heat the oil to 300°F (149°C) over medium heat.

Cut off both ends of the plantains. Using a knife, score each one lengthwise and release them from the peel. Slice the plantains crosswise into 2-inch (5 cm) lengths.

Working in batches, fry the plantains until they are a light golden brown. Remove them from the oil. While the next batch is frying, flatten the pieces from the previous batch between 2 pieces of parchment paper using a small frying pan (we use a tortilla press).

Heat the oil to 350°F (177°C).

Return the flattened plantains to the oil and fry until they are golden brown and crispy around the edges but the center is still a little soft. Transfer to paper towels to cool and season with *sal de chapulín*.

MAKE THE GUACAMOLE:

Preheat a grill (barbecue) or a cast-iron grill pan (griddle pan) to very high heat.

In a small bowl, combine the lime juice, avocado oil, and citric acid (if using). Season the avocados with salt and pepper. Brush them liberally with the lime juice mixture.

Place the avocado halves flesh side down on the grill until they are slightly charred, about 4 minutes. Flip them and grill on the skin side for 1–2 minutes to heat the avocados through but not char the skin. Remove from the grill and brush the flesh side with more lime juice mixture. Set aside to cool to room temperature.

Squeeze the avocado flesh into a large molcajete or bowl. It should slip right out of the skins from the grilling. Add the onion, jalapeños, cilantro (fresh coriander), cumin, olive oil, and any remaining lime juice mixture from the grilling process.

Process with the *mano* if in the molcajete or with a spoon in the bowl to get a semi-smooth paste with some small chunks about the size of a pea. Season with salt and pepper.

Serve immediately, with the freshly fried *tostones* for dipping. Guacamole can be stored in a pastry bag or airtight container for up to one day.

Rabbit Liver Mousse with Mesquite Toast

WE HAVE A HUMAN BEING who seasonally raises rabbits for us. While not entirely legal at this time (which is why I have declined to mention this human's name or even gender), I find it to be a much cleaner and more humane way of procurement than current lawful options allow. Part of the deal is that we are required to participate in the slaughter and butchery every two weeks during the season, which lasts for about six weeks in early spring. The quality of the lifestyle of these *conejos* shines through in their pristine livers. This is the only time we serve this dish.

Serves 6

2 lb (910 g)	fresh rabbit livers
2 tbsp (30 g)	cold organic butter
1 cup (160 g)	finely diced white onion
2 tsp	English thyme, minced
1 tsp	Himalayan pink salt
½ tsp	freshly ground black pepper
4 tbsp	Gran Patrón Tequila Extra Añejo Piedra
1 cup (240 ml)	cold organic heavy (whipping) cream
¾ cup (180 ml)	cold-pressed coconut oil, melted and fragrant
36 pieces	Mesquite Toast (page 169)
6	Pickled Quince (page 224), sliced in three lengthwise

With a very sharp paring knife, carefully remove the gall bladders and any connective tissue from the livers.

In a heavy-bottomed pan, heat the butter over medium heat. Add the onion and sauté until translucent but not browned, about 5 minutes. Increase the heat to medium-high and add the livers and thyme. Stir and cook until the livers are opaque but still medium, or pink, inside, about 6 minutes. Remove from the heat and let cool slightly.

Using a silicone spatula, transfer entire contents of the pan to a food processor and add the salt, pepper, and tequila and puree. Strain through a chinois or fine-mesh sieve, cover, and refrigerate while you whip the cream.

In a bowl with an electric mixer, whip the cream to soft peaks. Fold one-half of the whipped cream into the rabbit liver mixture to lighten it, then fold in the remainder. Adjust the seasoning with salt and pepper to taste.

Scrape the rabbit liver mousse into individual containers of your choice (we use 4 oz/120 ml Weck jars) that will hold it with space above it (the mousse should come up three-quarters of the way). Refrigerate for 1 hour or more to solidify. Cover with a layer of ¼ cup (60 ml) of the coconut oil. Refrigerate again so that the coconut oil hardens.

When ready to serve, remove the individual containers of mousse from the refrigerator and allow to temper for 1 hour. Serve individually potted mousse with the mesquite toast and pickled quince.

Seven-Layer Yucca Dip

ONE OF MY FAVORITE EVENTS is a dinner we host every year in Marfa during the Agave Festival. Bettina and I were trying to imagine dishes that represented our microcosm and/or microclimate. Three varieties of yuccas, my favorite being the Spanish Dagger, were in full bloom in our gardens and we were eager to do something interesting with them. I started talking about traditional seven-layer dip, which consists of beans, sour cream, guacamole, salsa, cheese, green onions, and canned black olives. Feeling very hungry and a little bit silly, this is what we came up with.

Serves 6

2 tbsp	avocado oil
1 lb (500 g)	fresh yucca buds, stems removed
	Kosher salt and freshly ground black pepper
1 lb (500 g)	yucca flowers, petals only (stems and stamens removed)
3½ tbsp	fresh lime juice
6 tbsp	Yucca Jam (page 218)
6 tbsp	finely chopped Pickled Yucca Blossoms and Buds (page 218)
6 tbsp	chopped Fermented Yucca Buds and Flowers (page 219)
6 tbsp	Dehydrated Yucca Petals (recipe follows)

In a frying pan, heat the oil over medium heat. Add the yucca buds and sauté until translucent, about 4 minutes. Transfer the buds to a plate or sheet pan and season with salt and pepper. Let cool to room temperature, then finely chop.

Meanwhile, in a bowl, toss the petals with the lime juice and season with salt.

To assemble the dip, spread the yucca jam in the bottom of a casserole dish, about 1–2 inches (2.5–5 cm) deep and 6–8 inches (15–20 cm) in diameter with a matching lid. Next, make an even layer of the pickled blossoms and buds over the jam. Layer an equal amount of sautéed buds over that, followed by a layer of the fermented yucca. Layer an equal amount of lime-dressed yucca petals over that. Set aside 1 tablespoon of the dehydrated yucca petals for smoke (see next step) and finish the dip with an equal amount of dehydrated petals.

At serving time, place the lid on the casserole and use the reserved tablespoon of dehydrated yucca petals in a smoking gun to pump in a layer of smoke. Serve immediately.

DEHYDRATED YUCCA PETALS
Makes 1 quart (1 liter) dry flowers

4 lb 6 oz (2 kg)	yucca flowers, petals only (stems and stamens removed)

Arrange the petals on dehydrator trays in even layers. Set the dehydrator temperature between 98°F (37°C) and 113°F (45°C) and dehydrate for 12 hours. Store in an airtight container. Although we live in the desert, we include a silica packet to insure dryness.

Prickly Pear–
Poached Pear

THERE ARE A LOT OF pear trees in Marfa—in our neighbors' yards, on abandoned lots, and some even in back alleys. In the fall we are either gifted the fruit or we go out and do a little urban foraging/scavenging. Originally I thought that a poached pear might be a little boring or old fashioned, but we made it more interesting by using spices and flavorings indigenous to the Americas, local honey, and our homemade prickly pear wine. It also turns out to have a very vibrant hue.

Serves 6

1 tsp	citric acid
6	firm-ripe pears, preferably from your neighbor's tree or Anjou
4¼ cups (1 liter)	Prickly Pear Wine (page 228) or your favorite Malbec
1½ cups (500 g)	honey, preferably catclaw or your favorite local variety
1	Mexican cinnamon stick
5	whole cloves
1	vanilla bean, split lengthwise

In a large bowl or plastic container, combine 4¼ cups (1 liter) water and the citric acid. Peel the pears and place them in the acidulated water as you work.

In a large pot, combine the wine, honey, cinnamon, and cloves. Scrape the vanilla seeds into the pot and add the pod. Bring to a simmer over high heat. Add the pears and simmer until tender and easily pierced with a knife, about 25 minutes. Remove from the heat and let the pears cool in the cooking liquid.

Remove the pears to a serving platter. Strain the poaching liquid through a fine-mesh sieve and return to the pot. Bring the liquid to a boil over medium heat and cook until it is reduced to the consistency of maple syrup, about 15 minutes. Spoon over the pears and serve.

Huauzontles

FIVE YEARS AGO WE BECAME members of Native Seeds/Search, a seed-saving nonprofit, and I ordered and planted some Hopi Amaranth. Unlike its green Mexican cousin, it comes in a bright crimson, similar to the color of red beets. With the help of the Marfa winds, it has self-seeded every year and grows like wildfire in the desert. *Huauzontle* is the Mexican name for amaranth and is also the name of a traditional preparation: The flowers and tender leaves are dipped in an egg batter and deep-fried with a salty chunk of cheese sandwiched within and then served with a thick red salsa. Inspired by this preparation, we tried to lighten it up and subtracted the cheese and tempura-fried the *huauzontles* instead.

Serves 6

6 tbsp	amaranth seeds
	Soybean oil, for deep-frying
2 cups (275 g)	cake flour
2 tbsp	tapioca flour
1 tbsp	mesquite powder, store-bought or homemade (page 203)
2½ cups (590 ml)	club soda (soda water), very cold
24	Hopi amaranth flower heads (3–4 inches/7.5–10 cm long)
24	Hopi amaranth leaf bundles
	Pink Himalayan salt

FOR SERVING

4	tomatillos, husked, and each sliced into 16 wedges
24	small and tender Hopi amaranth leaves
	Diamond Crystal kosher (flaked) salt
1	lime, quartered, central pith sliced off
1 cup (240 ml)	Recado Negro (page 212)
12	tortillas of your choice (see page 162)
½ cup (120 ml)	Salsa Pasilla (page 210)
24	sunflower petals

Heat a 4-quart (4-liter) saucepot over medium-high heat. Add 2 tablespoons of the amaranth seeds, cover, and shake until you hear the seeds popping. Pour the popped amaranth out onto a sheet pan and repeat with the remaining amaranth seeds, 2 tablespoons at time. Trying to pop it all at once creates too much steam and won't allow the amaranth to pop, leaving it to burn on the bottom of the pan.

Pour 4 inches (10 cm) of soybean oil into a deep-fryer or deep heavy pot. Heat the oil to 350°F (177°C).

Sift together the cake flour, tapioca flour, and mesquite powder into a bowl. Pour all of the cold club soda (soda water) into the flour mixture and stir with the fingertips of your dominant hand just until the batter comes together and there are no dry spots, 10–15 times. Do not overmix.

Working in batches of 8–10, dredge the amaranth flower heads and leaf bundles in the batter and immediately drop into the fryer while constantly stirring the oil with a spoon. Once they are evenly browned, 3–4 minutes, remove from the fryer and place on a cooling rack or paper towels to drain. Season immediately with Himalayan salt. When all the flower heads and leaves have been fried, set aside 6 of the finest-looking flower heads and cut the rest into 1-inch (2.5 cm) pieces.

TO SERVE:

In a small bowl, toss the tomatillos and small amaranth leaves with kosher salt and a squeeze of lime.

Divide the *recado negro* among 6 plates. Place upon this 1 reserved flower head and 2 tortillas slightly overlapping. Dress each tortilla with a spoonful of pasilla. Arrange the cut *huauzontles* and fried leaves on the tortillas. Garnish each with the dressed tomatillos and amaranth leaves, the sunflower petals, and popped amaranth. We serve this at room temperature because it is generally pretty hot around amaranth season, when this dish is typically on the menu.

"Peruvian" Potatoes

THE "PERUVIAN" IN THE TITLE comes from our respect and understanding that all potatoes originated in Peru. We were once gifted a variety of pristine and lovely fresh new potatoes. Inspired by the potatoes, and fortunately having some other things in the pantry, we set out to make a dish that attempted to honor and showcase the potatoes. Here's what it is: Imagine that you are at a somewhat refined Southern lunch and everyone gets drunk and starts arguing. A food fight ensues, and everyone leaves in a huff. You are the last human standing in the aftermath of that maelstrom, and you see that the chips and dip have spilled over into the potato salad. So as not to dishonor the host, or let anything go to waste, you must have a bite and instantly find yourself screaming aloud, "Whence was the caviar thrown?" It was such a short time we had with those potatoes and I always remember the plate looking like a mess but tasting like something magical.

Serves 6

12 oz (340 g)	crème fraîche
½	large white onion, finely chopped
5 lb (2.25 kg)	fingerling potatoes, assorted varieties
2 cups (270 g)	kosher (flaked) salt
	Neutral oil, for deep-frying
	Himalayan sea salt

FOR SERVING

2	shallots, cut into ⅛-inch (3 mm) slices, rings separated, soaked in ice water
4	scallions (spring onions), green tops only, thinly sliced
6 oz (170 g)	celery heart stalks, cut on the bias into ⅛-inch (3 mm) pieces
4 oz (115 g)	celery heart leaves
	Bottarga (preferably Gulf Coast Caviar brand), to taste
3	Cured Egg Yolks (page 220)
	Onion or Leek Top Ash (page 202)
	Salt and freshly ground black pepper

In a small bowl, combine the crème fraîche and onion. Refrigerate for at least 2 hours and up to 6. Strain the crème fraîche through a chinois or fine-mesh sieve and reserve in the refrigerator.

In a small stockpot, combine 3 pounds (1.35 kg) of the potatoes and 6 quarts (5.7 liters) water. Bring to a boil and add the kosher (flaked) salt. Reduce to a simmer and cook until the potatoes are cooked through but still hold their form, 15–20 minutes. Drain the potatoes, place on a sheet pan, and allow them to air-dry and form salt crystals on their skins. Trim the ends and cut the salt potatoes into roll-cuts. Reserve.

Meanwhile, pour 4 inches (10 cm) oil into a deep-fryer or deep heavy pot. Heat the oil to 300°F (149°C).

Using a meat slicer or mandoline, slice the remaining 2 pounds (910 g) potatoes lengthwise into slices ¹⁄₁₆ inch (1.5 mm) thick. Transfer the slices to a bowl of cold water as you work.

Working in batches of about 20, carefully fry the potato slices until golden brown or they stop bubbling in the oil, 4–5 minutes. Remove and drain on a cooling rack or paper towels and season lightly with Himalayan sea salt. Once cool, reserve in an airtight container.

TO SERVE:

Pool 4 tablespoons of the onion crème fraîche on each of 6 plates. Arrange the salt potatoes standing up or toppled over as you see fit. Judiciously garnish each plate with the shallots, scallion (spring onion) tops, celery stalks, and celery leaves. With reckless abandon, Microplane the bottarga and cured egg yolk over each plate. Then throw pinches of onion ash and salt, and finish with a grind of black pepper. Delicately place the fingerling chips and serve immediately.

A Windswept Salad of Every Lettuce, Soft Herb, Flower, and Edible Native Species in the Garden Today

THERE IS A BRIEF WINDOW in early spring/late summer during which we can get something from almost all of our native and cultivated plants in the garden, be it the first flowers, their full leaves, or their young seeds as they start to bolt. We pick everything and store each individually. While a blend can be visually stunning, our first priority in choosing ingredients is taste and texture, as well as representing the landscape fairly. This can be done with as many or as few ingredients as you have on hand. We call it "windswept" because the spring breezes help us with the plating, blowing flowers everywhere as the server carries the dish to the table.

Serves 6

6 quarts (6 liters) assorted lettuces, herbs, and flowers, in any combination of the following:

Agarita berries	Marigold flowers
Arugula (rocket) leaves	Mexican elderflowers
Baby romaine leaves	Mexican plum blossoms
Borage flowers	Mexican tarragon leaves
Calendula flowers	Nasturtium flowers
Chive blossoms	Pansy flowers
Cilantro (coriander) flowers	Parsley leaves
Columbine flowers	Purslane (verdolaga)
Desert willow flowers	Red sorrel leaves
Echinacea flowers	Red trumpet flowers
Epazote	Rosemary flowers
French breakfast radishes	Sorrel leaves
Honeysuckle flowers	Sunflower petals
Hopi amaranth leaves	Tatsoi flowers
Lovage leaves	Yucca blossoms

¾ cup (175 ml)	Catclaw Honey and Lime Vinaigrette (page 215)
	Coarse sea salt (such as Maldon, or sel gris)
	Freshly cracked black pepper
2	limes, quartered, central pith sliced off
3 tbsp	extra virgin olive oil
3 tbsp	aged balsamic vinegar (optional)

Separate the salad fixings by type (see below) and place in 3 bowls.

For the leaves, dress lightly with vinaigrette, making sure the leaves are lightly and evenly lubricated, and salt and pepper.

For the herbs and sturdier flowers, dress lightly with fresh lime juice and olive oil.

For the most delicate flowers, do not dress.

Combine the dressed leaves, herbs, and flowers however you see fit on a large platter, or divided among 6 plates. Add the undressed flowers. Garnish the salad with sea salt and cracked pepper and drizzle with balsamic (if using).

Sopa de Guias with Chochoyotes

THIS DISH WAS INSPIRED BY one of Abigail Mendoza Ruiz's signature dishes at her restaurant Tlamanalli in Teotitlán del Valle. One year, we had tons of pumpkins and squashes growing so we wanted to use every part of the plant and make a light summer soup. I love the delicate flavor and the look of the dish. It also makes me laugh because when we make it I always want to call it Mexican Matzo Ball Soup, because the *chochoyotes* are little round masa balls floating in broth. Masa, matzo...whatever.

Serves 6

FOR THE BROTH

20	pumpkin or squash vines, each about 18 inches (46 cm) long, roughly chopped
20	pumpkin or squash leaves, roughly chopped
1	large white onion, cut into eighths
1	head garlic, halved horizontally
1	bunch epazote, leaves only
1	bunch English thyme sprigs
	Kosher (flaked) salt and freshly ground black pepper

FOR THE CHOCHOYOTES (DUMPLINGS)

1 cup (250 g)	tamale masa (page 128, using water in place of mushroom broth), at room temperature
6	squash blossoms, petals only, stamens reserved, finely chopped
8	marigolds, petals only, finely chopped

FOR SERVING

12	largish pumpkin or squash leaves
3	young and tender pumpkin or squash vines, 6–8 inches (15–20 cm) long, thinly sliced
24	tiny pumpkin or squash leaves
6	squash blossoms, petals and stamens separated
12	pumpkin or squash clinging tendrils
18	baby pumpkin or squash fruits or buds

MAKE THE BROTH:

In a stockpot, combine the vines, leaves, onion, garlic, and 3 quarts (3 liters) water and bring to a boil. Reduce to a simmer and cook for 20 minutes. Remove from the heat and add the epazote and thyme. Allow the herbs to steep and the broth to cool for at least 1 hour. Strain through a chinois or fine-mesh sieve and season very lightly with salt and pepper.

MAKE THE CHOCHOYOTES (DUMPLINGS):

In a small saucepan, bring 4 cups (1 liter) of the broth to a slow simmer.

Place the masa dough in a bowl and use your hands to combine the chopped flowers with the dough until it forms a cohesive mixture. Using a #100 scoop (about 2 teaspoons) or your good judgment, divide the dough into generous 1-inch (2.5 cm) balls. Make an indention in each one using your thumb or index finger.

Add the *chochoyotes* to the simmering broth and once they float allow them to cook for 2 minutes. Scoop out and set aside. Combine the dumpling poaching liquid with the original broth and strain through a chinois or fine-mesh sieve.

TO SERVE:

Bring the broth to a boil. Add the *chochoyotes* to heat up.

On each of 6 plates, place two pumpkin or squash leaves as underliners. Place 6 heated bowls on top of the leaves. Into each bowl ladle 1¼–1½ cups (295–355 ml) of the broth and 3 *chochoyotes*. Garnish with sliced vines, tiny leaves, squash blossom petals, tendrils, buds, and reserved stamens.

Watermelon Radishes with Habanero Vinegar, Aged Balsamic, and Lime

WHEN WE FIRST STARTED SERVING food in the bar at the Capri it was the end of January and the only vegetables we had growing were watermelon radishes. Combined with pickled watermelon rind and habanero vinegar from the previous summer it turned out to be a spicy and textural treat with a striking presentation. Save your watermelon rind for pickling and the rest of the flesh for eating (or make the gazpacho on page 110).

Serves 6

6	watermelon cubes (2½ inches/6.5 cm), from the watermelon heart
	Kosher (flaked) salt
1	lime, quartered, central pith sliced off
3	medium watermelon radishes, peeled and cut into ⅛-inch (3 mm) slices
3 tbsp	habanero pickling liquid (see page 220)
4 tbsp	aged balsamic vinegar
24	pieces Pickled Watermelon Rind (page 225)

In a small bowl, dress the watermelon cubes with salt and squeeze in the juice of 2 lime quarters. In a separate bowl, dress the radish slices with salt, habanero vinegar, and the juice of the remaining 2 lime quarters.

Divide 2 tablespoons of the balsamic across 6 plates as droplets. Arrange the radish slices on the plates like a carpaccio. Make a divot in the watermelon cubes using a small melon baller. Place the cube slightly off-center, in the northwest quadrant of each plate or wherever you think looks nice, and fill the divots with the remaining balsamic. Scatter 3-5 pieces of the pickled watermelon rind over each plate of radishes as you see aesthetically fit.

Capri Crudités

THIS IS AN ASSORTMENT OF fresh vegetables that are on hand depending on the season. The original inspiration for this humble dish was our first visit to the tiny restaurant stall eponymously called Doña Maria in the Mercado de Benito Juárez in Ciudad Oaxaca. At Doña Maria, the proprietress keeps the lights off during the day, service is prompt, and all the spoons in her *cazuelas* always point the same way. The food has been lovingly and laboriously prepared and sits in *cazuelas* on the counter.

Upon sitting, guests immediately receive a tiny wooden boat with fresh veggies and herbs, including radishes, avocados, guaje beans, and *chepiche*, with pepitas, *sal de gusano*, and lime on the side to dress and dip them *al gusto*. When we are feeling nostalgic and vitamin-deficient, and the season is right, we try to rekindle a little bit of all of that. This recipe can be divided into as many or as few serving bowls as you choose. It is engineered for six bowls, which can serve quite a few. Our friend Daniel Humm, the chef at Eleven Madison Park in New York City, who also keeps all of his houses neat as a pin, and who also is not afraid to serve a little crudités, serves his in snow; so feel free to try that if the season is appropriate.

Serves 6

12	French breakfast radishes
24	baby carrots from the garden, washed and trimmed
12	celery hearts, yellow parts only
2	pomegranates, roughly split into quarters
2	avocados, pitted but unpeeled, sliced into eighths
24	sprigs purslane (verdolaga)
18	squash blossoms, petals and stamens separated
18	asparagus tips, 3 inches (7.5 cm) long
18	broccoli florets, blanched 1 minute then shocked
18	cauliflower florets, blanched 2 minutes then shocked
18	Romanesco florets, blanched 2 minutes then shocked
1	Armenian or English (seedless) cucumber, cut into matchsticks
1	jicama (yam bean), cut into matchsticks
24	cremini (chestnut) mushrooms, quartered
12	scallions (spring onions), roots removed, cut down to 4 inches (10 cm) in length
12	serrano peppers, sliced in half lengthwise
4	limes, quartered, center pith sliced off
12	guaje bean pods, half of the pod peeled off, leaving the beans exposed
1½ cups (355 ml)	Recado Negro (page 212)
	Sal de Chapulín (page 202) or sal de gusano, for serving

Fill 6 bowls with crushed ice. Place a small sauce bowl (at the restaurant we use a *jícarito*, a small gourd) in the center of each one and fill them with ¼ cup (60 ml) of *recado negro*. Artistically arrange the crudités ingredients and sprinkle the *sal de chapulín* as liberally and wherever you wish.

Chicharrón

IN MARKETS ACROSS MEXICO THERE are butcher's stalls where you can buy not only a piece of pig, but also chicharrones, fried pig skin, to snack on while you do your shopping. In the US we're used to seeing petite pork rinds as snack food, but in these market stalls they're more likely to fry the skins in huge sheets. Inspired by the butcher stalls and the people frying chicharrones in the various markets, we set out to make the big ones. Although not terribly difficult, cooking twenty-five pounds of pork skin can be an arduous task. Also, our kitchen smelled like pig skin for weeks. So we ultimately scaled it back. With that in mind, if you require any more than what this recipe yields, I recommend going to a Mexican market or grocery that is large enough to be making them fresh every day.

Serves 6 a gracious plenty

1½–2 lb (680–910 g)	pork belly skin
	Soybean or peanut oil, for deep-frying
	Kosher (flaked) salt
	Gochugaru (Korean red chili flakes)
	Salsa Pasilla (page 210), for serving
	Raw Salsa Verde (page 211), for serving
	Lime wedges, for serving

Place the pork skin in a large pot and add water to cover by 4 inches (10 cm). Bring to a boil, then reduce to a simmer and cook for 2 hours.

Remove the pork skin and lay it flat on a wire rack or dehydrator tray. Place in an oven set to 180°F (85°C) or a dehydrator set to 145°F (63°C). Allow the pork skin to dry for at least 8 hours. Remove the pork skin and scrape/wipe away any residual fat, leaving only the dry skin.

To fry the skin whole, a very large pot is needed, preferably over a burner outdoors. And you will need a great deal of oil: about 10 quarts (10 liters). Or break the skin into smaller pieces and use a deep-fryer or deep heavy pot. Either way, the pork skins expand dramatically.

If deep-frying in pieces, pour 6–8 inches (15–20 cm) oil into a deep-fryer or deep heavy pot. Heat the oil to at least 400°F (204°C). Submerge the pork skin and fry until fully expanded, bubbly, and crisp, 3–4 minutes. Remove from the oil and season with salt and gochugaru.

Serve with salsa pasilla, salsa verde, and fresh limes. We like to serve the whole chicharrón for dramatic effect and let the humans sort it out with their hands.

Favas "In Their Shoes" with Pumpkin Seed Pesto

I HAVE A NOTE THAT I wrote to myself so many years ago that I do not know when I wrote it or why I have it. I have referred to it only twice, counting right now. It is obviously from a cookbook and I do not know whom to credit. It reads, "Habas en Zapatadas/Fava Beans in their shoes/Guatemala City." Following this quote is a recipe for fava beans (broad beans) that are cooked all night, so they do not have to be peeled, and one can imagine that tastes pretty good. Fava beans are of Spanish origin rather than being indigenous to Central America. In addition to growing in protective pods, the individual fava beans are also armored by thick skins. When eating them, each diner traditionally squeezes the beans out of the rather tough skins and deposits the skins on a plate. These are the "shoes" of the beans."

In our second year at the Capri some things happened that ended with me finally making this recipe: We were inundated by human beings asking why we did not serve fava beans; Virginia demanded to know what was so hard about serving fava beans; fava beans all of a sudden started growing in the garden without my knowledge of them being planted; and Bettina, the only other cook at the time, demanded to make fava beans. I had to imagine that maybe subconsciously I was afraid of the favas and had been tortured as a youth by having to peel fava beans—a common preparation for cooking the beans in fine-dining establishments. I realized this was not true, because I found it terribly exciting, when I was a very young cook, to be handling something so exotic while on my path to becoming a professional. I also understood that we were on our third year of trying to reintroduce the Chihuahuan tepary bean, one of the ancestors of all true legumes that exist. The poor thing is drought-resistant and it rained like hell and everyone was too busy looking at the fava beans.

The favas came in. They came in in the garden and they came in the back door. Some survival synapse fired in my brain and I remembered the favas in their shoes. We served the sautéed young pods and only peeled the favas that needed it and served the others in "their shoes." Bettina is still traumatized that her fava bean dream came true.

Serves 6

3 lb (1.35 kg)	fava (broad) bean pods, inconsistent sizes are fine
¼ cup (60 ml)	fresh lemon juice
¾ cup (175 ml)	extra virgin olive oil
¼ cup (60 ml)	avocado oil
½	white onion, finely diced
3	garlic cloves, minced
	Diamond Crystal kosher (flaked) salt and freshly ground black pepper
½ cup (35 g)	chopped flat-leaf parsley
1 cup (240 ml)	Pepita Vinaigrette (page 208)
½ cup (65 g)	hulled pumpkin seeds, toasted
	Grated zest of 2 lemons
6	marigolds, petals only

Reserving the pods, pull the fava (broad) beans out of their pods. String the pods, then slice them crosswise into ¼-inch (6 mm) lengths. Set the beans aside.

In a small bowl, stir together the lemon juice and olive oil.

In a large frying pan or wok, heat the avocado oil over high heat. Add the pods and stir-fry until cooked through and slightly browned, about 3 minutes. Reduce the heat to medium and add the onion and garlic. Cook until translucent but not browned, 4–5 minutes. Season with salt and pepper. Remove from the pan and spread onto a sheet pan to cool. Once cool, season with half of the lemon juice/olive oil mixture and half of the parsley. Set aside.

Set up a large bowl of ice and water. In a large pot, bring 6 quarts (6 liters) water to a boil and add 1 cup (135 g) kosher (flaked) salt. Add the beans and blanch for 3–4 minutes, then shock in the ice bath. Drain well and divide the beans into two piles: smallish and largish. Peel the larger ones.

In a bowl, combine both sizes of beans and season with salt and pepper to taste. Dress with the remaining lemon juice/olive oil mixture and the parsley.

Dress each of 6 plates with 2 tablespoons of pepita vinaigrette followed by 2 spoons of sautéed fava pods and 2 spoons of dressed fava beans. Garnish with toasted pumpkin seeds, lemon zest, and marigold petals.

Yucca Blossom Tempura

THIS WAS ONE OF OUR first offerings of yucca blossoms. They came in in force that year, and having no frame of reference for what to do with them, we served them tempura-fried with *chiltomate*—a spicy cooked tomato sauce that can be served warm or cold. Inadvertently we made Chihuahuan Calamari.

Serves 6

	soybean oil, for deep-frying
2 cups (275 g)	cake flour
2 tbsp	tapioca flour
1 tbsp	mesquite powder, store-bought or homemade (page 203)
2½ cups (590 ml)	club soda (soda water), very cold
4 qt (4 liters)	yucca blossoms (about 50), stems and stamens removed
	Pink Himalayan salt
	Chiltomate (page 205, optional) for serving
	Prickly pear reduction (optional), for serving
	Gochugaru and lime quarters (optional), for serving

Pour 4 inches (10 cm) oil into a deep-fryer or deep heavy pot. Heat the oil to 350°F (177°C).

Sift together the cake flour, tapioca flour, and mesquite powder into a bowl. Pour all of the cold club soda (soda water) into the flour mixture and stir with the fingertips of your dominant hand 10–15 times. Do not overmix.

Working in batches of 8–10, dredge the yucca blossoms in the batter and immediately drop into the fryer while constantly stirring. Once they are evenly browned, remove from the fryer and place on a rack or paper towels.

Season immediately with Himalayan salt and serve. We serve these with any one of these accompaniments: Chiltomate (page 205), prickly pear reduction, or gochugaru (Korean red chili flakes) and lime.

Watermelon Gazpacho with Tequila, Sal de Gusano, and Aged Balsamico

WHEN I WAS LITTLE I used to get in trouble for eating the very central heart of the watermelon, because I had learned that it was the sweetest part, before anyone else could get to it. I still like to serve *el corazón de sandia* seasoned with lime juice, *sal de chapulín*, and a little tamarindo or balsamic. With the remaining flesh we make this simple gazpacho, and we turn the rinds into pickles.

Serves 6

1 generous cup (200 g)	coarsely chopped heirloom tomato
2 tbsp	chopped serrano pepper
2 lb (1 kg)	watermelon, peeled and chopped
3 tbsp	red wine vinegar
1 cup (150 g)	chopped red onion
2 cups (250 g)	chopped peeled cucumber
½ tsp	xanthan gum
	Kosher (flaked) salt and freshly ground black pepper
½ cup (20 g)	cilantro (fresh coriander), tied in cheesecloth for steeping

FOR SERVING

6	2-inch (5 cm) cubes watermelon
¼ cup (60 ml)	tequila blanco
1	lime, quartered
	Sal de Chapulín (page 202) or sal de gusano
	Aged balsamic vinegar, such as Balsamico Villa Manadori
12	garlic chives

In a high-powered blender, combine the tomato, serrano, watermelon, red wine vinegar, red onion, cucumber, and xanthan gum and puree. Season with salt and pepper. Pass through a chinois or fine-mesh sieve. Add the cilantro (fresh coriander) sachet and refrigerate for 1–4 hours. Remove the sachet and pour the mixture into the canister of an iSi whip and charge 2 times. Chill for an additional 2 hours. (Alternatively, serve the gazpacho without charging and additional chilling.)

TO SERVE:

Make a divot in each watermelon cube with a medium melon baller. Dress each cube with tequila, lime juice, and *sal de chapulín* to taste. Fill the divot in each cube with balsamic. Attach 2 garlic chives like rabbit ears to the sides of each cube.

Place a watermelon cube in each of 6 chilled bowls, and divide the gazpacho among the bowls. Serve immediately.

Fire-Roasted Pumpkin Soup with Soft Masa

THERE ARE CERTAIN DISHES AND ingredients I have been mulling over and repurposing for the past twenty years that I've been cooking professionally. This dish feels like the perfect distillation of a bunch of things that I love. Although it's a soup, take my word for it that its current incarnation feels a bit like Mexican Shrimp and Grits.

Serves 12

FOR THE PUMPKIN SOUP

1	12–16 pound (5–7 kg) cheese pumpkin
4 tbsp	avocado oil
1	large white onion, finely diced
4	garlic cloves, minced
	Kosher (flaked) salt and freshly ground black pepper

FOR THE SOFT MASA

4 cups (950 ml)	whole organic milk
	Pinch of cayenne pepper
½ cup (65 g)	cornmeal
½ cup (142 g)	prepared masa (page 160)
½ cup (45 g)	grated Parmigiano-Reggiano cheese
4 tbsp (60 g)	cultured butter
1	sneaking suspicion grated nutmeg
	Kosher (flaked) salt and freshly ground black pepper
12	eggs, fresh from the coop
12	slices (⅛ inch/1.5 mm thick) La Quercia Prosciutto Americano
2 tbsp (30 g)	butter
6	trumpet royale (king trumpet) mushrooms, halved, face side scored
	Sea salt
2 tbsp	organic cold-pressed coconut oil, melted
18	Gulf shrimp (prawns; 20/25 count), peeled and deveined, halved lengthwise
3 tbsp	finely chopped cilantro (fresh coriander)
2	lime quarters
	Sea salt and freshly cracked black pepper, for serving
¾ cup (175 ml)	pumpkin seed oil, for serving

MAKE THE PUMPKIN SOUP:

Light a fire in a Big Green Egg or other covered grill of your choice, and dampen the fire to 300°F (150°C). Or preheat the oven to 300°F (150°C/Gas Mark 2). Place the pumpkin in the grill overnight allowing the fire to burn out. Or roast in the oven, until the pumpkin is steaming, soft to the touch, and beginning to collapse, 2–3 hours. Peel and seed the pumpkin.

In a soup pot, heat the avocado oil over medium heat. Add the onion and garlic and cook until translucent, about 5 minutes. Add the pumpkin and just enough water to cover (about 2 quarts/2 liters). Bring to a simmer and cook for 30 minutes. Puree in a high-powered blender and season to taste with salt and pepper. Hold in a water bath to keep warm.

MEANWHILE, MAKE THE SOFT MASA:

In a large saucepan, combine the milk and cayenne and bring to a slow simmer. Whisk in the cornmeal, then the masa, and then the Parmigiano. Using a wooden spoon or silicone spatula, stir in the butter and season with the nutmeg and salt and black pepper to taste. Hold in a water bath to keep warm.

Set a sous vide immersion circulator to 63.5°C. Lower in the eggs and leave for 1 hour. Turn the circulator down to 57°C for holding the eggs.

Preheat an oven to 300°F (150°C/Gas Mark 2). Line 2 half-sheet pans with silicone liners. Lay the prosciutto out on the lined pans and bake until the prosciutto is crispy, 18–20 minutes. Place in an airtight container between layers of paper towels.

In a frying pan, heat the butter over high heat. Add the mushrooms cut sides down. When the mushrooms begin to brown, turn them over for 30 seconds. Season with sea salt, remove from the pan, and set aside.

In a sauté pan, heat the coconut oil over medium-high heat. Season the shrimp with salt and pepper. Add to the pan and sauté until the flesh is opaque, 2–3 minutes. Stir in the cilantro (fresh coriander) and squeeze in the juice from the limes.

To serve, in each of 12 individual warm bowls, place 2 spoons of warm masa. Sauce around this with the pumpkin soup. Crack the eggs one at a time into a slotted spoon, allowing a small amount of uncoagulated white to slough off. Place in the center of the warm masa. Scatter 3 shrimp halves around the egg along with 1 mushroom half and 1 slice crispy prosciutto. Season the egg with sea salt and pepper. Drizzle 2 tablespoon of pumpkin seed oil around the dish.

Composed Dishes

I understand the relief we seek through comfort food, that which is certain and recognizable. At the Capri, we try to balance the use of more unusual ingredients with the familiarity of dishes like a giant proper steak from cattle raised right here in Texas. We need some certainty in life.

Anchos Rellenos
de Guajolote

WE DEVELOPED THIS RECIPE OVER the course of two years. It seems like a simple chile relleno, the kind you can get anywhere north or south of the border, however a lot of thought and subtle changes occurred to get to this point. Instead of fire-roasted poblanos, we use toasted ancho chiles. Anchos are dried poblanos and we wanted to concentrate the flavor. I had been traveling around Mexico and wanted to bring a balanced mix of concentrated flavors to a traditional dish. There is no batter and no frying. The filling is a mixture of inspirations from the Mennonites of the Chihuahuan Desert to the Zapotecs grinding mole in Oaxaca to the clean, sweet fragrance of the Yucatán.

Serves 6

12	ancho chiles
	Boiling water, for soaking
3 tbsp (35 g)	lard
2½ lb (1.13 kg)	ground (minced) turkey, preferably organic
½	large white onion, finely diced
6	garlic cloves, minced
3	plantains, peeled and cut into medium dice
5	serrano peppers, seeded and finely diced
2 tbsp	dried Mexican oregano
1 tbsp	ground cumin
2 tsp	ground allspice
2	Mexican cinnamon sticks
2	bay leaves
5½ cups (48 oz/1.36 kg)	canned whole peeled San Marzano tomatoes
2 tbsp	white sesame seeds, toasted
½ cup (75 g)	dried currants
8 oz (225 g)	queso Menonita, diced, plus 6 oz (170 g) cut into 12 slices (Monterey Jack can substitute)
1	bunch cilantro (fresh coriander), chopped
	Salt and freshly ground black pepper
About 12 tbsp	Salsa Pasilla (page 210)

In a dry frying pan or on a comal, toast the anchos over medium heat until fragrant, turning once, about 2–3 minutes per side. When cool enough to handle, remove the seeds and place the chiles in a heatproof bowl. Add boiling water to cover and let soak for 1 hour.

Meanwhile, in a large frying pan, heat the lard over medium-high heat. Add the ground (minced) turkey and cook, breaking up the meat with a spoon or spatula, until browned, about 20 minutes. Add the onion, garlic, plantains, and serranos and continue cooking until the chiles are soft and the onions are translucent, about 10 minutes.

Add the oregano, cumin, allspice, cinnamon sticks, bay leaves, and tomatoes and bring to a simmer. Cook, stirring occasionally, until the mixture is cohesive and all residual water has evaporated, almost like Bolognese, about 30 minutes. Remove the pan from the heat and stir in the sesame seeds and currants. Allow to cool for 30 minutes.

When the turkey mixture is cool, fold in the diced cheese and the cilantro (fresh coriander). Taste and season with salt and pepper. Transfer the mixture to a bowl or plastic container and refrigerate for at least 2 hours.

Preheat the oven to 350°F (180°C/Gas Mark 4).

Drain the anchos of their soaking water. Remove the filling from the refrigerator, taste, and adjust the seasoning if necessary. Fill the chiles through the split in their sides until they are full and plump (but not bursting at the seams) and resemble fresh peppers again. Place the filled anchos on a sheet pan and bake for 7 minutes. Remove from the oven and place a slice of cheese on each one. Return to the oven and bake until the cheese is melted, about 3 minutes.

Remove from the oven and preheat the broiler (grill). Place the anchos rellenos under the broiler to brown the cheese (or use a kitchen torch).

On a serving platter or 6 individual plates, spread the salsa pasilla using a small palette knife or spoon. Set the rellenos on the pasilla and serve immediately.

Camarones Divorciados

HUEVOS DIVORCIADOS IS A TRADITIONAL dish in Mexico that is red salsa and green salsa on a plate with fried eggs in the center dividing the two salsas, keeping them separated, or "divorced." The dish is also evocative of the red, white, and green stripes of the Mexican flag. We replicate this in our own way using fermented red and green salsas and replacing the eggs with shrimp scented with smoldering fig leaves.

Serves 6

30	Gulf shrimp (prawns, 20/25 count), peeled and deveined, tails on
6	yucca or bamboo skewers
1	head garlic, halved horizontally
½ cup (120 ml)	extra virgin olive oil
3 tbsp	organic cold-pressed coconut oil, melted
	Kosher (flaked) salt and freshly ground black pepper
3 tbsp	finely chopped cilantro (fresh coriander)
½	lime, halved, central pith sliced off
1½ cups (355 ml)	Fermented Red Sauce (page 214)
1½ cups (355 ml)	Fermented Green Sauce (page 215)
6	fig leaves, central ribs removed

Thread 5 shrimp on each of the skewers. Place in a Cryovac bag with the garlic and olive oil. Vacuum-seal at 100%. (Alternatively, place in a shallow pan or zippered plastic bag.) Refrigerate on ice and allow to marinate for 2–4 hours or up to overnight.

In a large frying pan, heat the coconut oil over medium-high heat. Season the shrimp skewers on both sides with salt and pepper. Place the skewers in the pan and cook until the flesh is opaque, 2–3 minutes on each side. While in the pan, season them with the cilantro (fresh coriander) and squeeze the juice of 2 lime quarters over them. Remove from the pan.

Spread ¼ cup (60 ml) each of the red and green sauces onto each of 6 plates. Remove 1 shrimp from each skewer and place the skewer with the remaining shrimp down the middle between the 2 sauces. Tuck the single shrimp in randomly. Layer a fig leaf on top and burn slightly with a kitchen torch to make it smolder a bit.

Camarones Recado Negro

RECADO NEGRO IS YUCATECAN IN origin and possibly the mother of all moles. Traditionally the ingredients are all indigenous and roasted until blackened but not necessarily burned. Depending on the chiles used, it can be as spicy as you like. It can also be thick or thin, hot or cold, and used as seasoning, stuffing, sauce, or salsa. This versatility and heat drew us to create our own versus simply following other more traditional mole recipes.

Serves 6

30	Gulf shrimp (prawns, 20/25 count), peeled and deveined, tails on
6	yucca or bamboo skewers
1	head garlic, halved horizontally
½ cup (120 ml)	extra virgin olive oil
3	medium watermelon radishes, peeled and spiralized
	Kosher (flaked) salt
3 tbsp	habanero pickling liquid (see page 220)
1	lime, quartered, central pith sliced off
3 tbsp	organic cold-pressed coconut oil, melted
	Freshly ground black pepper
3 tbsp	finely chopped cilantro (fresh coriander)
1 cup (240 ml)	Recado Negro (page 212)
½ cup (125 g)	Store-bought wakame seaweed salad

Thread 5 shrimp on each of the skewers. Place in a Cryovac bag with the garlic and olive oil. Vacuum-seal at 100%. (Alternatively, place in a shallow pan or zippered plastic bag.) Refrigerate on ice and allow to marinate for at least 4 hours or up to overnight.

In a bowl, dress the radish slices with salt, habanero vinegar, and the juice of 2 of the lime quarters.

In a large frying pan, heat the coconut oil over medium-high heat. Season the shrimp skewers on both sides with salt and pepper. Place the skewers in the pan and cook until the flesh is opaque, 2–3 minutes on each side. While in the pan, season them with the cilantro (fresh coriander) and squeeze the juice of the remaining 2 lime quarters over them. Remove from the pan.

Divide the *recado negro* among 6 plates. Place the dressed, spiralized radishes down the center of each plate. Remove 1 shrimp from each skewer and place the skewer on the side of the radishes and tuck the single shrimp into the radishes. Garnish with wakame seaweed.

Zacahuil

A *ZACAHUIL* IS A GIANT tamale, measuring anywhere from 1–5½ yards (1–5 meters) long, traditional to the Huastec people on the Gulf Coast of Mexico. *Zacahuiles* are cooked in huge earthen ovens and can feed 50 to 150 people, depending on the size. In different parts of the region, people use whatever leaves are native to the area as a wrapper for the massive tamale; they can be corn husks, banana leaves, chaya, camoxchitl, canek, or hawaiana to name a few. I am forever inspired by the squash vine and blossom soup that chef Abigail Mendoza Ruiz serves at her restaurant Tlamanalli in Oaxaca. One year we planted a mess of 4,000-year-old native squash and pumpkin varieties, and to celebrate them we made our own version of *zacahuil* using everything from the calabazas. This is that recipe, which we still serve when the squash are in season. For the poached squash, use any variety of *Cucurbita moschata* or *C. maxima*, but preferably *C. moschata*. If using *C. maxima*, choose Hubbard or kabocha.

Serves 6

FOR THE POACHED SQUASH

3	slices squash of your choice (see note): ½ inch (1.25 cm) thick, trimmed into 3 × 4-inch (7.5 × 10 cm) rectangles, scored in a crosshatch pattern
1 tbsp	kosher (flaked) salt
1 tbsp	homemade duck jus reduction or store-bought demi-glace
1 tbsp	juice from Pickled Muscat Grapes (page 225)
1 tbsp	fresh lime juice

FOR THE SQUASH LEAF BASE

20	squash or pumpkin vines around 18 inches (46 cm) each, roughly chopped
20	squash or pumpkin leaves, roughly chopped
	Kosher (flaked) salt and freshly ground black pepper

FOR THE SQUASH LEAF SAUCE

Generous ½ tsp	xanthan gum
3 tbsp	Versawhip
1 tbsp	Stabiwise (stabilizer)

POACH THE SQUASH:

Season each squash rectangle with the salt and rub it in. Vacuum-seal the slices with the duck jus, pickled grape juice, and lime juice at 100%. Set a sous vide immersion circulator to 82.7°C and poach the squash for 30 minutes. Chill in an ice bath and reserve.

MAKE THE SQUASH LEAF BASE:

In a large pot, combine the squash vines, squash leaves, and 3 quarts (3 liters) water. Bring to a boil, then reduce to a simmer and cook for 10 minutes. Remove from the heat and season lightly with salt and pepper. Transfer to a blender and puree. Pass through a chinois or fine-mesh sieve. Divide the squash leaf base in half. Reserve.

MAKE THE SQUASH LEAF SAUCE:

In a high-powered blender, combine 900 g or half of the squash leaf base with the xanthan gum, Versawhip, and Stabiwise and process on the highest setting. Reserve.

(continued)

FOR THE SQUASH LEAF PAPER

3	egg whites
1 tsp	kosher (flaked) salt
½ tsp	freshly ground black pepper

FOR THE ZACAHUIL FILLING

3 tbsp	avocado oil
1	white onion, finely diced
4	garlic cloves, minced
1 tbsp	dried Mexican oregano
1 tsp	ground cumin
12	squash or pumpkin vines and leaves, about 18 inches (46 cm) each, roughly chopped
6–8	heirloom tomatoes, cored, cut into medium-small dice
	Kosher (flaked) salt and freshly ground black pepper

FOR THE TAMALE MASA

6 oz (170 g)	lard
1 tsp	baking powder
2 tsp	kosher (flaked) salt
2 lb (910 g)	prepared masa, store-bought or homemade (page 160)

MAKE THE SQUASH LEAF PAPER:

In a high-powered blender, combine the remaining one-half squash leaf base with the egg whites, salt, and pepper. Process to a puree. Pass through a chinois or fine-mesh sieve. Line 2 half-sheet pans with silicone baking liners. Spread the mixture evenly, about an ⅛ inch (3 mm) thick, onto the liners.

Place in the dehydrator at 143°F (62°C) until the "paper" easily comes loose from the liners, 2–3 hours. Break the sheets into pieces and store in an airtight container with silica packets.

MAKE THE ZACAHUIL FILLING:

In a medium saucepan, heat the avocado oil over medium heat. Add the onion and garlic and cook until translucent but not browned, about 5 minutes. Add the oregano, cumin, squash vines, and tomatoes. Cook until most of the residual water has evaporated, about 10 minutes. Season with salt and pepper.

Set the filling in a chinois or fine-mesh sieve set over a bowl and allow to drain for 20 minutes. Transfer the solids to a blender and puree. Reserve the liquid in the bowl for the tamale masa (below).

MAKE THE TAMALE MASA:

In a stand mixer fitted with the paddle, combine the lard, baking powder, and salt and beat on medium-high speed for 2 minutes. With the mixer running, add the masa a little at a time and then adjust the texture with the liquid reserved from the *zacahuil* filling. The final masa should be light and fluffy.

FOR ASSEMBLY

20	squash or pumpkin leaves, blanched and shocked, stored between paper towels

FOR THE PUMPKIN/PUMPKIN SEED SALSA

½ cup (115 g)	diced (⅛ inch/3 mm) pumpkin or squash
½ cup (65 g)	hulled pumpkin seeds, fresh and tender
½ cup (85 g)	thinly sliced squash or pumpkin vines
1 tbsp	habanero pickling liquid (see page 220)
2 tbsp	fresh lime juice
	Kosher (flaked) salt and freshly ground black pepper

FOR SERVING

2 tbsp	avocado oil
6	squash blossoms, petals and stamens separated
¾ cup (175 ml)	homemade duck jus reduction or store-bought demi-glace

ASSEMBLE THE ZACAHUIL:

Using a wet towel, moisten the surface of a stainless steel table or countertop. Cover with a sheet of plastic wrap (cling film) 18 × 24 inches (46 × 61 cm). Arrange a layer of approximately 10 blanched leaves into a shape 15 × 13 inches (38 × 33 cm) on the plastic. Spread a layer of tamale masa about 13 × 10 inches (33 × 25 cm) and ⅜ inch (9.5 mm) thick.

Spoon half of the filling down the center of the *zacahuil*. Using the plastic wrap, roll the *zacahuil* into a tight cylinder and twist the ends in opposite directions. Using another sheet of plastic wrap, repeat the twisting process to have a tightly sealed cylinder. Repeat with the remaining leaves, masa, and filling.

Set a sous vide immersion circulator to 82.7°C or bring a pot of water to a bare simmer. Add the *zacahuils* and poach for 1 hour. Remove and refrigerate.

MAKE THE PUMPKIN/PUMPKIN SEED SALSA:

In a bowl, combine the diced pumpkin, pumpkin seeds, slices vines, vinegar, and lime juice. Season with salt and pepper. Set aside.

TO SERVE:

Preheat the oven to 400°F (200°C/Gas Mark 6).

Unwrap the *zacahuiles* and cut each one into 6 equal slices. Slice the poached squash in quarters on the diagonal.

In a cast-iron frying pan, heat the avocado oil. Place the *zacahuil* slices and poached squash slices in the pan and place in the oven for 5–6 minutes.

In the center of 6 plates, spoon about ¼ cup (60 ml) of the squash leaf sauce. Smack the sauce with a spoon to splatter it on the plate. Spoon some of the pumpkin seed salsa onto the plate. Remove the *zacahuil* and squash slices from the oven and place 2 *zacahuil* slices and 1 squash slice on each plate. Garnish with a piece of squash leaf paper and a squash blossom.

Finish each plate with 2 tablespoons of duck jus.

The Capri Steak

IF YOU OPEN A ROADSIDE saloon on the Mexican border in Texas cattle-ranching country, you really don't have a choice whether you are going to serve a steak. When we first opened the Capri there were only two of us total kitchen staff and the plating room had much less fire power than it does now. Back then we had one countertop convection oven, one induction burner, one sous vide machine, and one torch. Now we have two of each! Although we do have a larger prep kitchen in the back and what we call "the man cage," where the BBQ pit and outdoor grills reside, it's a long skateboard ride back and forth to be cooking steaks the traditional way so we developed this method. It has turned out to be shockingly consistent and good. It's a little too popular, but that's okay. We still have ranchers who come in a little suspicious, saying, "I heard you serve one of the best steaks in the world, but I don't smell no fire burning," but they always leave as converts. The next step was sourcing quality beef that we could get consistently. We currently use Akaushi beef, originating from Beeman Ranch in Harwood, Texas, by way of Japan. Fun fact number one: Harwood is just north of Virginia's family ranch, which is outside of Victoria, Texas. Fun fact number two: Our friend Jim Dyer, a local rancher, came in to try our steak. He introduced himself and his lovely wife and informed me that he raises 20 percent of the Akaushi beef produced in our neighboring town of Valentine. I am always trying to get him to just drop one of those steers off on their way through town—"for the sake of efficiency!" I say. (The steers have to be shipped to slaughter at a facility inspected by the US Department of Agriculture and it would be illegal for me to slaughter a cow in the backyard and serve it to our guests.) He has a great sense of humor and just laughs at my ignorance of how ranching works.

Serves 4

1	bone-in ribeye (46–52 oz/1.3–1.5 kg), preferably Akaushi
	Kosher (flaked) salt and freshly ground black pepper
2	limes, quartered, central pith sliced off
2 tbsp	Sal de Chapulín (page 202) or sal de gusano
2 tbsp	gochugaru (Korean red chili flakes)

Preheat the grill of your choice to very high.

Generously season the steak with salt and pepper. Place on the grill for 1 minute. Give the steak a quarter turn and grill for 1 minute more. Turn the steak over and repeat the process on the other side. Remove from the grill and allow to cool.

Vacuum-seal the steak. Set a sous vide immersion circulator to 57°C and cook the steak for at least 1 hour, but it can go for as long as 5 hours.

When you are ready to serve, preheat the oven to 450°F (230°C/Gas Mark 8).

Remove the steak from the bag, reserving the cooking liquid. Place the steak on a rack on a sheet pan and roast for 3 minutes. Remove from the oven and sear both sides of the steak with a kitchen torch to the desired level of brown and crustiness. Allow to rest for 3–5 minutes.

Slice the steak and place on a board or platter. Serve with the reserved jus from the bag and limes dipped in *sal de chapulín* and gochugaru.

Tamales Vaporcitos Yucatecos With Salsa Pasilla

ONE SUMMER IT RAINED A lot more than we are accustomed to and some of the plants in the garden took off disproportionately. We had lots of shiso, borage, and *verdolaga* (purslane). At the same time we were talking seasonality of tamales and vegan dishes and waiting on a shipment of proper lard from happy pigs. We had also just received samples of non-GMO corn that originated in southern Mexico but that had been grown in Texas. None of this makes very much sense, but Bettina was able to take off with the weirdness and we made masa out of the corn, made tamale dough with coconut oil instead of lard, and made a filling inspired by the garden. This became three variations of vegan tamales. We call the tamales Yucatecos because we steam them in banana leaves, rather than corn husks, which is how they do it in the Yucatán.

Makes 12 tamales
FOR THE TAMALE MASA

¾ cup (175 ml)	organic coconut oil
2½ tsp	salt
2 tsp	baking powder
2 lb (910 g)	prepared masa, store-bought or homemade (page 160)
1 cup (240 ml)	mushroom soaking liquid from Borage and Shiitake Tamale Filling (recipe follows) or water

TO FINISH

	Choice of filling (recipes follow)
1 or 2	large fresh banana leaves
	Salsa Pasilla (page 210), for serving

MAKE THE TAMALE MASA:

In a stand mixer fitted with the paddle attachment, combine the coconut oil, salt, and baking powder and beat on high. With the mixer running, slowly add the masa until incorporated. Slowly add the mushroom soaking liquid and mix until fluffy. Cover and refrigerate for 1 hour. When ready to use, remove from the refrigerator and let come to room temperature.

TO FINISH:

Make the filling of choice. Cut the banana leaves into 6-inch (15 cm) squares. Spoon 3 ounces (85 g) masa dough into the center of each banana leaf square. Spoon 2 ounces (55 g) of filling into the center of the dough. Fold the tamale into a neat package and set aside fold side down. You can also tie them with kitchen twine or a strand of banana leaf.

In a tamale steamer or a bamboo steamer, steam the tamales for 1½ hours. Let rest for 30 minutes before serving.

Serve with salsa pasilla.

BORAGE AND SHIITAKE TAMALE FILLING
Makes 1½ pounds (680 g)/enough for 12 tamales

½ cup (120 ml)	extra virgin olive oil
1	large white onion, finely diced
8	garlic cloves, minced
1 lb (455 g)	borage leaves and stems, chopped
4 cups (150 g)	dried shiitakes, soaked to rehydrate, drained, liquid reserved, and finely diced
	Kosher (flaked) salt
	Gochugaru (Korean red chili flakes)
6 oz (170 g)	queso Menonita, finely diced

In a large frying pan, heat the olive oil over medium-high heat. Add the onion, garlic, borage, and mushrooms and cook until soft, about 5–6 minutes. Season with salt and gochugaru. Fold in the queso Menonita when cool.

POBLANO AND HIBISCUS TAMALE FILLING
Makes 1½ pounds (680 g)/enough for 12 tamales

½ cup (120 ml)	extra virgin olive oil
2	white onions, finely diced
8	garlic cloves, minced
9	poblano peppers, fire-roasted, peeled, seeded, and chopped
6	dried chipotle peppers, soaked to rehydrate, seeded, and chopped
3	dried hibiscus flowers, soaked to rehydrate and chopped
¼ cup (60 ml)	perilla oil
	Kosher (flaked) salt

In a large frying pan, heat the olive oil over medium heat. Add the onions, garlic, poblanos, and chipotles and cook until onions are translucent, about 8 minutes. Stir in the hibiscus, perilla oil, and salt to taste.

SHISO AND PURSLANE TAMALE FILLING
Makes 1½ pounds (680 g)/enough for 12 tamales

½ cup (120 ml)	extra virgin olive oil
2	white onions, finely diced
8	garlic cloves, minced
9	poblano peppers, fire-roasted, peeled, seeded, and chopped
30	dried shiitakes, soaked to rehydrate, drained, and finely diced
2 cups (50 g)	chopped shiso leaves
2 cups (80 g)	chopped purslane (verdolaga)
3	dried chipotle peppers, soaked to rehydrate, seeded, and chopped
3	dried pasilla chiles, soaked to rehydrate, seeded, and chopped
3	ancho chiles, soaked to rehydrate, seeded, and chopped
3	dried guajillo chiles, soaked to rehydrate, seeded, and chopped
¼ cup (60 ml)	perilla oil
	Kosher (flaked) salt

In a large frying pan, heat the olive oil over medium-high heat. Add the onions, garlic, poblanos, and mushrooms and cook until soft, about 10 minutes. Add the shiso and purslane. Fold in the chipotles, pasillas, anchos, and guajillos. Stir in the perilla oil and season with salt.

Muscovy Duck

WHEN THE FIRST "SETTLERS" ARRIVED in Mesoamerica, there were four domesticated animals: the dog, the turkey, the Muscovy duck, and the cochineal. Further south there were llamas, alpacas, and guinea pigs. We like to give a little salute to the duck, and although the cooking techniques are slightly French in tradition, the flavors and ingredients are New World–inspired and work harmoniously down to the bitter cacao and pungent marigolds that are anything but an afterthought. We use whole ducks for this recipe and cook the breasts and legs simultaneously with different preparations (confit for the legs, pan-seared for the breasts). On the menu we alternate between the two, but at home you can do either or both.

Serves 6

FOR THE CONFITED DUCK LEGS

6	duck legs
	Kosher (flaked) salt and freshly ground black pepper
	Achiote Paste (page 204)

FOR THE SEARED DUCK BREASTS

6	duck breasts
	Kosher (flaked) salt and freshly ground black pepper
6 tbsp	cumin seeds

FOR SERVING

1 cup (240 ml)	Salsa Huitlacoche (page 212)
2 cups (475 ml)	Curtido (page 226)
6	cacao beans
6	marigolds, petals only
2 limes	quartered, central pith sliced off
2 tbsp	gochugaru (Korean red chili flakes)

MAKE THE CONFITED DUCK LEGS:

Season the duck legs on both sides generously with salt. Only season the flesh sides with pepper. Place on a rack on a sheet pan in the refrigerator uncovered for at least 2 hours.

Remove the duck legs from the refrigerator and brush off any excess salt. In a mixing bowl rub the duck legs down with the achiote paste. Vacuum-seal the duck legs. Set a sous vide immersion circulator to 76°C. Cook the duck for at least 8 and up to 10 hours.

MAKE THE SEARED DUCK BREASTS:

Preheat a cast-iron frying pan over medium heat. Trim the duck breasts of any silverskin or excess fat. With a very sharp knife, score a crosshatch pattern on the skin side, exposing the subcutaneous fat but not going down to the flesh. Season both sides of the breasts with salt and pepper. Sprinkle 1 tablespoon of cumin seeds on the skin side of each breast and lightly rub in.

Place the duck breasts skin side down in the heated cast-iron pan with no additional fat. Leave them, allowing the fat to render, until the skin is a crisp and golden brown, 9–12 minutes. The heat might need adjusting periodically. Turn the breasts over and allow to cook on the flesh side until medium rare, 5–6 minutes. Remove from the pan and reserve.

TO SERVE:

Preheat the oven to 400°F (200°C/Gas Mark 6).

Place the duck confit or duck breasts on a rack in a sheet pan and roast for 7–8 minutes.

Smear 2 tablespoons salsa on each of 6 plates. Divide the curtido among the plates in even piles.

If serving breasts: After removing from the oven, allow to rest for 5 minutes. Briefly flash the skin with a kitchen torch and slice into 5 pieces and plate.

If serving the confit: After removing from the oven, sear the skin with a kitchen torch until golden brown and crispy. Place on the plate.

Garnish the duck by shaving an entire cacao bean over each dish, sprinkling marigold petals on each one, and placing a lime dipped in gochugaru and a steak knife alongside.

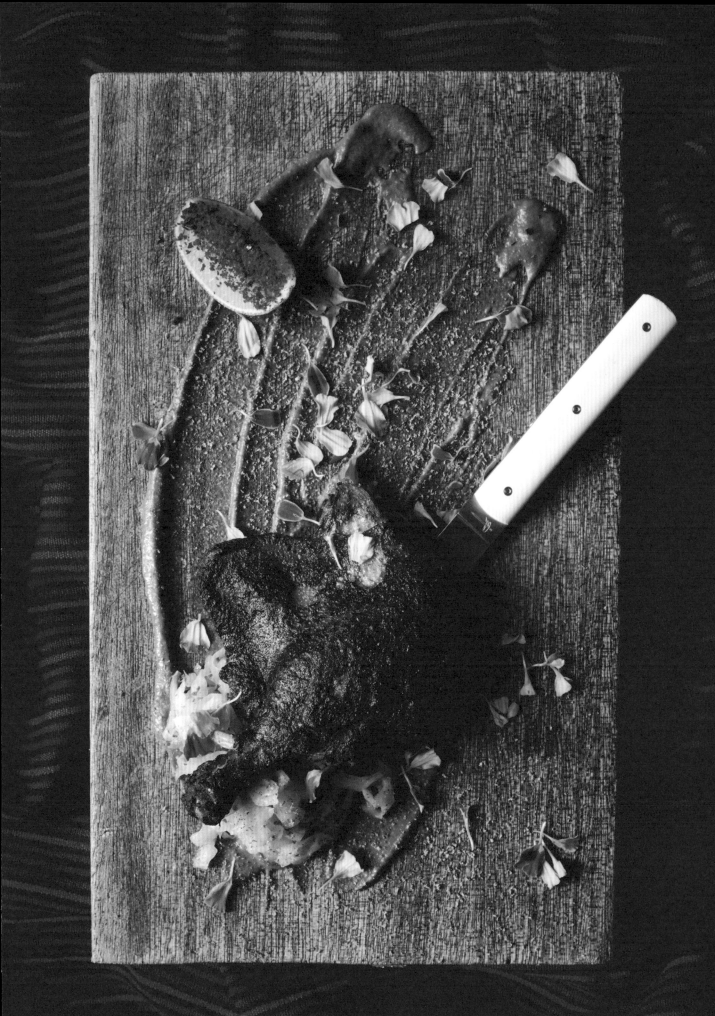

Our Rabbits Braised in Our Prickly Pear Wine

THIS IS A FAIRLY SIMPLE rendition of braised rabbit that depends on a culmination and concentration of flavors straight from our little piece of Hell's Half Acre out here. We feed and slaughter the rabbits, we pick the prickly pears from specific patches and carefully ferment the wine, and we pick the herbs straight from the garden prior to cooking, sometimes neglecting to knock all the dirt off. Accordingly, you won't really be able to re-create this dish unless you're in Marfa, and if that's the case you might as well come eat it at the Capri. But if you need a technique for braising rabbit, this is a solid starting place. Just substitute your favorite nice quality wine, like Beaujolais Nouveau or Malbec, for the prickly pear juice and wine.

Serves 6

3	whole rabbits, store-bought or freshly slaughtered, dressed, and aged 3 days in the refrigerator
	Kosher (flaked) salt and freshly ground black pepper
¾ cup (175 ml)	cold-pressed coconut oil, melted and fragrant
3	heads garlic, halved horizontally
12	sprigs French thyme
8½ cups (2 liters)	Prickly Pear Wine (page 228)
3	bay leaves, preferably from Louise O'Connor's ranch
1 cup (240 ml)	fresh prickly pear juice
1 cup (225 g)	lightly salted cultured butter

Preheat the oven to 400°F (200°C/Gas Mark 6).

Remove the legs and forelegs from the rabbits. Remove the loins and reserve for another use. Place the carcasses on a sheet pan in the oven to roast until browned, 30–40 minutes. Remove the browned carcasses to a stock pot and fill with water to cover. Bring to a simmer over medum-high heat then reduce heat to medium low. to maintain simmer. Partially cover and cook stock for 2½ hours. Strain the stock through a fine-mesh sieve set over a large bowl or medium pot. Discard solids and reserve stock.

Meanwhile, season the rabbit legs generously with salt and pepper.

In a wide shallow pot, heat the coconut oil over medium-high heat. Add the garlic cut side down and cook until golden brown, about 5 minutes. Add the thyme during the last 2 minutes and fry to infuse the oil. Remove the thyme and garlic and reserve.

Add the rabbit legs to the pan and cook until golden brown on each side. Pour in the prickly pear wine, add the bay leaves, and return the garlic and thyme to the mixture. Bring to a slow simmer, cover, and simmer until the legs are tender but not falling apart, 1½–2 hours.

Remove the legs from the liquid and place them on a rack to cool. Strain the cooking liquid and return to a pot. Add the reserved rabbit stock and prickly pear juice and cook to reduce to a saucelike consistency, about 20 minutes. Strain through a chinois or fine-mesh sieve.

When ready to serve, heat the rabbit legs in the reduced sauce and then remove and place them on 6 individual plates or 1 serving dish. Over low heat, whisk the butter into the sauce, adjust the seasoning with salt and pepper, and spoon the sauce over the rabbit.

Tostadas al Carbon with Razor Clams and Chorizo

WHILE MAKING VARIATIONS ON TORTILLAS one day I made a black one by adding activated charcoal. In Mexico, anything cooked over charcoal is referred to as *al carbon*. We had been wanting to make something with clams and chorizo, so we decided to serve them on a *tostada al carbon* to lend the charcoal flavor. The spirulina echoes the flavor of the sea and ties it all together.

Serves 6

FOR THE GREEN DUCK CHORIZO

1 lb (455 g)	skin-on duck breast
1 tbsp	coriander seeds
1 tsp	black peppercorns
4	whole cloves
⅛ tsp	cumin seeds
1	bay leaf
¼ tsp	dried Mexican oregano
8	garlic cloves, roughly chopped
2	serrano peppers, roughly chopped
1	poblano pepper, roughly chopped
¼ cup (60 ml)	prickly pear vinegar or sherry vinegar
1 cup (75 g)	chopped flat-leaf parsley
1 tbsp	Diamond Crystal kosher (flaked) salt

FOR THE TOSTADAS

12	tortillas (page 162), made with activated charcoal
½ cup (120 ml)	cold-pressed coconut oil, melted, plus more for brushing
2 lb (910 g)	razor clams, 4–5 inches (10–12.5 cm) long, washed in cold water and drained
¼ cup (60 ml)	avocado oil
2	heads garlic, halved horizontally
10	dried avocado leaves
½ cup (120 ml)	Tequila Extra Añejo
2 tsp	spirulina powder (preferably Blue Majik)
1 cup (40 g)	Mexican Mint Marigold leaves

MAKE THE CHORIZO:

Cut the duck breast into 1-inch (2.5 cm) cubes and refrigerate to keep cold before grinding.

On a comal or in a frying pan over medium-high heat, combine the coriander, peppercorns, cloves, and cumin seeds and toast. Set aside to cool.

In a large bowl, combine the duck, toasted spices, bay leaf, oregano, garlic, serranos, poblano, vinegar, parsley, and salt and mix well. Put the mixture through a meat grinder fitted with a coarse plate. Take half of the ground mixture and process through a medium plate. Mix the medium grind with the coarse grind and cook a small amount to taste. Adjust seasoning with salt if necessary. Refrigerate until use.

MAKE THE TOSTADAS:

Preheat a comal or the oven to 300°F (150°C/Gas Mark 2). Brush both sides of the tortillas lightly with coconut oil. Toast the tortillas on both sides on the comal or in the oven until dry and crispy. Reserve.

Meanwhile, in a wide shallow pot with a lid, heat the coconut and avocado oils over medium-high heat. Add the garlic heads, cut sides down, and cook until blackened and fragrant, about 4 minutes. Immediately add the razor clams, avocado leaves, and tequila. Cover tightly and let steam for 5–6 minutes. Remove the clams from the pot and place on a sheet pan to cool. Pour the cooking liquid through a chinois or fine-mesh sieve and cool. When the clams are cool, remove them from their shells and slice them crosswise into ½-inch (1.25 cm) pieces. Combine with the cooking liquid and vacuum-seal at 100%. Refrigerate under ice.

To serve, preheat the oven to 350°F (180°C/Gas Mark 4). In a dry cast-iron frying pan, brown the chorizo over medium-high heat.

Lay the tostadas on a sheet pan. Divide the cooked chorizo and clams evenly among them. Place in the oven for 5–7 minutes. Remove from the oven and place on plates or platters and throw spirulina and Mexican Mint Marigold at them.

Masa Pasta Ravioli with Cured Egg Yolks and Gulf Bottarga

THIS RECIPE CAME ABOUT WHEN Bettina and I were trying to figure out how to make masa pasta. Our intention was to make pasta that had the same texture as pasta but the flavor of masa. We tried fresh masa, corn flour, and Maseca in differing ratios until we finally nailed it with this recipe. Our friend Mary Farley came in and brought us eggs from her geese. I imagined a pretentious recipe for fun: *Goose Egg Masa Pasta Ravioli Filled with the Still-Warm Egg Yolks from Our Hens, Air-Cured Egg Yolks, and Gulf Bottarga; Egg on Egg on Egg on Egg.* We toned it down and came up with something better.

Serves 6

2 cups plus 3 tbsp (283 g)	all-purpose (plain) flour
2⅓ cups (283 g)	Maseca or masa harina, plus more for dusting
4	whole eggs
18	egg yolks
2	egg whites
2 tbsp	avocado oil
1 cup (80 g)	tiny green amaranth florets, blanched and shocked
1 tbsp	gochugaru (Korean red chili flakes)
	Diamond Crystal kosher (flaked) salt and freshly ground black pepper
8 oz (225 g)	Parmigiano-Reggiano cheese

FOR SERVING

1 cup (240 ml)	Squash Leaf Pesto (page 210)
¼ cup (60 ml)	extra virgin olive oil
	Kosher (flaked) salt and freshly ground black pepper
3	Cured Egg Yolks (page 220)
	Bottarga, preferably Gulf Coast Caviar brand
4 tbsp	English thyme leaves
4 tbsp	desert willow flowers

In a food processor, pulse together the flour and Maseca. With the machine running, add the whole eggs and, if needed to form a dough, up to ¼ cup (60 ml) water. When it combines and forms a ball, remove and knead by hand for 5–7 minutes to develop the protein (gluten) structure. Cover with plastic wrap (cling film) and let rest in the refrigerator for at least 1 hour.

Divide the pasta dough into 4 portions. Progressively run each portion through a pasta machine ending with sheets at the number 2 setting.

Lay a sheet on a work surface that has been dusted with Maseca. Place half of the egg yolks 3 inches (7.5 cm) apart in a line down the center of one of the pasta sheets. Using the egg whites, brush a circle 2 inches (5 cm) in diameter around each egg yolk. Top with another sheet of pasta and use the dull (unfluted) side of a 2½-inch (6.5 cm) fluted ring cutter to press the pasta down around the egg yolk sealing it in. Use your fingers to press around the sealed egg yolk sealing the sheets of pasta together. Cut out the ravioli with the fluted side of the cutter and place them on a sheet pan dusted with Maseca and allow to air-dry for 15 minutes. Cover and refrigerate.

Meanwhile, in a frying pan, heat the avocado oil over high heat. Quickly sauté the amaranth and season with the gochugaru and salt and pepper to taste. Drain on paper towels. Reserve.

TO SERVE:

Bring a large pot of salted water to a rolling boil.

Using a Microplane, carpet six individual plates with a layer of Parmigiano-Reggiano. Place 2 spoons of squash leaf pesto in the center of each plate.

Add the ravioli to the boiling water and cook for exactly 2 minutes. Drain and dress with olive oil, salt, and pepper.

Place 3 ravioli on each plate and scatter the amaranth florets around. Garnish with Microplaned cured egg yolks and bottarga, the thyme leaves, and desert willow flowers.

The Cuisine Of the Capri

If you dig deep enough into the history of the plate in front of you, it can ignite your understanding of ecology, botany, war, drought, trade routes, technology, and social structures. Food and culinary endeavors are magical art forms, ones that can take you far beyond the basic need for sustenance.

A MAGICAL ART   by Virginia

When I first arrived in Marfa, there were three main restaurant options—Mando's, Borunda's, and Carmen's—all serving variations on Chihuahuan Desert Tex-Mex food. In fact, legend has it that the first Tex-Mex restaurant in Texas was started right here in Marfa in 1887 by Tula Borunda Gutierrez. They say that Miss Tula was the creator of Tex-Mex cuisine as we know it. She took basic Mexican ingredients and added to them to suit the tastes of ranchers, railroad workers, and her community of neighbors. Thus a culinary fusion of mythological proportions started right here in Marfa.

The fourth option was Maiya's, opened in 2002 by Maiya Keck, who to my knowledge was the first person to introduce a new cultural culinary influence into Marfa. She opened an Italian restaurant. This was an absolute game-changing endeavor for the town, for the locals who chose to be patrons, and for the tourists coming through. There have since been ebbs and flows and shifts that have taken place with restaurants over the years, each one felt mightily. Even when a restaurant closes and another opens, the Earth undulates slightly with the anxiety produced by change in a tremendously small town. Mando's is the only one of these four restaurants from my early days in Marfa that is still open and still on its original path. By the time we started talking about opening the Capri, there were eleven or so establishments serving food throughout the day, on most days except Monday and Tuesday, not including the gas stations. The Capri was our effort to add one more layer to the options where people might land and rock up in the evening hours; we wanted to bring some variation to what was then available for sustenance and culinary experiences in Marfa.

It was Rocky's beautiful idea to focus as much as possible on the region, the landscape, and our proximity to Mexico as points of inspiration for the menu. Additionally, finding fresh produce out here has always been a struggle. However, from struggle comes creativity. Or as Rocky likes to say,

"A lack of options clears the mind."

So we have reached to the land, uncultivated, to find the jewels that give the rich locality to the menu. We appreciate living in a region so austere it makes you giddy and wide-eyed to hold a locally raised vegetable, which someone else grew, and in quantities plentiful enough for this old roadside saloon. They are, indeed, like jewels, and we are acutely aware of how precious they are. We also wanted to create a menu that required us to explore and learn from our environment and the multiplicity of cultures existing around us. As Rocky began to explore the cacti, mesquite beans, and flowers of the desert, I started thinking about the regional equivalent in design and history of rural watering holes of the past.

I understand the relief we seek through comfort food, that which is certain and recognizable. At the Capri, Rocky tries to balance the use of more unusual ingredients with the familiarity of dishes like a giant proper steak from cattle raised right here in Texas. We need some certainty in life. Here in Texas there is nothing like steak to provide a sense of place and a sense of calm. We can push cultural boundaries, but not too far. That would just be rude.

However, I always experience a sense of wonder when food and drink challenge me to understand a cultural tradition, an ingredient, or a process I did not grasp before that moment. For example, we serve cheese and honey produced by the large communities of Mennonites living in the Chihuahuan Desert in Northern Mexico near our border. These people, of both Dutch and Prussian ancestry, came to Northern Mexico by way of Canada in the 1920s after the Canadian government mandated regulatory assimilation of all children into government schools. The more conservative Mennonites declined to assimilate and instead negotiated a mass immigration plan with then Mexican President Álvaro Obregón.

These communities are vibrant and expansive. They look nothing like traditional or contemporary Mexican communities. Their homes are built in rural Dutch architectural styles and their Northern European propensities for tidiness and rigid order are evident in the midst of the gorgeous chaos

of modern-day Mexico. They produce traditional handmade queso meno-nita, a soft cow's milk cheese, and cultivate bees. We buy the cheese in huge rounds and the honey dripping from the combs and both have become integral to our menu at the Capri.

We also use *chapulines*, dried grasshoppers, in some dishes at the Capri as a reflection of our connection to the cultures of Mexico and to hope-fully coax our guests into experiencing a few of the culinary traditions that exist to the south of our border. *Chapulines* are a traditional culinary element from Southern Mexico, specifically Oaxaca. Before the Spanish conquest of Mexico and more broadly, Latin America, pigs, cattle, chickens, and horses were not indigenous to this part of the world; instead, insects were a major source of protein. In a world where grander cuts of more rec-ognizable (or more European) meats are expensive, the grasshoppers, ants, ant eggs, and worms are still elemental and necessary for the tradi-tional communities. *Chapulines*, however, are more difficult to acquire than the queso. Although you can order them online, that without question squashes the romance. We prefer to carry them in our suitcases from Oaxaca, where they are toasted on a hot comal over fire with a little salt and lime.

Huitlacoche, a fungus that grows on corn, is another example of these traditions. In some countries, entire fields would be burned if this fungus appeared. It would be considered an infestation, a plague. In Mexico, it is a delicacy. It is used in moles, soups … I suppose it is used anywhere one would consider using a mushroom. At the Capri, we have used it in moles for duck dishes. It has an earthy flavor and texture of mushrooms heavy with the scent of corn. To the unfamiliar eye it is visually slightly terrifying. It is almost black, and the enlarged kernels of corn filled with the fungal spores form patterns that look not unlike the human brain. It is delicious, yet wild and offbeat for many North American palates.

When we are out on the ranch in West Texas, we sometimes find ancient molcajetes in rock formations. Molcajetes in the landscape, cylinders ground into the boulders by grinding seeds, are usually found near sys-tems of caves where the indigenous people camped. They were the preamble to the European mortar and pestle, or the portable versions of molcajetes found in modern Mexican kitchens. At these sites, archeologists can study thousands of years of ash sediment from the fires of the people who camped in these places. Rocky and I dream of what it was like to survive, to eat before food was delivered by trucks or cultivated in garden patches.

There is one particular place on the ranch that we call the Shaman Site—a sacred place where people ingested peyote to achieve ceremonial fervor. There are grinding molcajetes there surrounded by jagged upright boulders that look like they fell from the sky. Carved into these boulders are intricate and far-out designs—petroglyphs. The images include what we call the Spaceman, a human figure with exaggerated and long undulating arms; something that looks like a rocket ship; and snake-like lines, compact and feverish, that feel like chaos and madness or maybe just the meditation that repetition brings.

The Capri is our contemporary version of a shaman site. It is a place for ceremony, where we gather at the fires we build in the bar and in the gardens and commune with nature and each other through the ancient rituals of shared sustenance and libations. Food and drink have always had the ability to illuminate the histories, struggles, victories, defeats, and cultural shifts that exist in a particular region or with a particular group of people. They can paint a picture of civilization from basic survival to utter opulence. If you dig deep enough into the history of the plate in front of you, it can ignite your understanding of ecology, botany, war, drought, trade routes, technology, and social structures. I think about food and culinary endeavors as magical art forms; ones that can take you far beyond the basic need for sustenance.

WE ALL
GOTTA EAT

by Rocky

My arrival in Marfa in December 2008 represented a dramatic change and a seismic shift in my life. People would often ask me how it felt to live in a small town in the middle of nowhere. What they didn't realize was that I had been working in Washington, Virginia, a town that was five blocks by two blocks and had a population of 187 humans. In comparison, Marfa, which is a one-mile (1.6 km) square and has a population of 1,800 humans, felt like a metropolis to me. In Rappahannock County, though, which is where Washington sits, the isolation takes the form of the rolling Blue Ridge Mountains and miles of farms. At the Inn at Little Washington, surrounded by this geographic and agricultural opulence, we had much more access to pristine seasonal ingredients and wild foods, but fewer dining options on a daily basis than even in Marfa. Moving to a slightly larger town in the middle of the Chihuahuan Desert was terribly exciting.

In the early days, or years, of my time in Marfa, the Food Shark food truck was parked in the middle of town and it felt like everyone wound up there just about every day at lunchtime. It was parked under a giant shade structure, and townspeople and tourists would file in, place their order, maybe go check the mail, and sit down at one of the oversized communal Judd picnic benches. It was the only place to consistently offer lunch that was not a fast-food restaurant, and it was there that everyone would not just eat, but meet and greet, and catch up on town news. It was also exciting for me at the time, having spent the majority of my life in a restaurant *serving* the humans, to be able to go somewhere to have lunch and even a civilized dinner *with* the humans.

We had the restaurants Maiya's, Cochineal, and the Hotel Paisano if one wanted to feel a little more upscale. Padres was a favorite watering hole that had the best cheeseburgers and boudin sausage, and the town was bookended by Mando's and Borunda's, the latter being a hideout of choice for some of us. You can pretty quickly make friends and, so as not to get tired of the local restaurant scene, people would take turns hosting dinner parties, and I particularly enjoyed this. After working day and night for so many years, it was nice to have a sense of normalcy, actually cooking in the home versus professionally in a restaurant. But then the townspeople inevitably turned on me, all with the same question:

"I heard you are a chef, when are *you* going to
open a restaurant?"

And they all relentlessly asked that question every day for years on end.

I felt like it was my civic duty as a new member of what I half-jokingly call a pioneer town, to cook for humans, but understanding the difficulties of restaurant ownership even in places with resources, I was not so inclined to open a restaurant. So I did anyway! Even though I did not have total confidence, the pressure from the townspeople and my desire to be an upstanding citizen made me cave in.

Through the first restaurant I opened in Marfa, Miniature Rooster, I learned a lot of things I needed to know about business, taxes, and liquor laws. This accrued wisdom became beneficial in consulting and helping other people who wanted to contribute a little food and drink to the town, too. I also learned that our original idea of trying to be inviting and inclusive to all the humans that patronized our establishment—be they ranchers, multi-generational members of the Latino community, newly established residents, or curious visitors—was a good idea. We always had a lively mix of humanity at the Rooster eating fried chicken and curry, and drinking canned beer.

This sort of universally appealing and welcoming attitude translated per-fectly to our idea of roadside saloon/mercantile/restorative situation at the Capri for inhabitants and visitors alike. Although it is most certainly hard to please all the people all of the time, and here at the crossroads we receive a very diverse cast of characters who all tend to be very opinionated.

The most daunting thing for a person trying to live out here, much less host guests and visitors, is a lack of resources. Although we sit on an aquifer of fresh water, have a very long growing season, and have loads of wild edi-bles to be rediscovered, things like food, water, upwardly mobile human beings capable of being gainfully employed, the ever-elusive Wi-Fi, and even the cellular service that has come to be considered a human right and basic need—these seem always to be in short supply. This is still the wild West in many ways. Coming here from Appalachia I recognized the self-sufficient nature of the human beings here, but there were far fewer farmers, foragers, and people living off the land than I was accustomed to (but never took for granted).

These challenges, and particularly the seeming lack of fresh produce in the area, were one of several key points of inspiration for me in my current commitment to a lifetime of learning about the inhabitants and the culture (most importantly what they ate) of our specific region, and more broadly the Americas.

Another of these inspirations has been my encounters with the early cultures of the land around Marfa. We often visit Virginia's mother's ranch seventy miles west of town, which has been set aside for remediation after previous owners had overgrazed the land. Bighorn sheep and prairie dogs, both native species that had almost disappeared, have been reintroduced, and you might even see a big cat if you are lucky. But the most interesting things for me are the pictographs in a boulder field, which we refer to as the Shaman Site, that are thousands of years old, and the caves and fire spots where human beings used to cook and live. Arrow points from the ranch have been dated as being over 10,000 years old. Seeing these precious clues and artifacts, sleeping in the caves under the stars, feeling this very specific energy, understanding that humans had traversed this land for thousands of years before Dairy Queen (for which I am eternally grateful), taking into account the change in weather patterns and the effects of industrialization—Virginia and I realized one day that we both had been asking the same question:

"What were they eating?"

So she recommended that I read *1491* by Charles C. Mann. This led to an epiphany. I did not really know as much as I needed to about my Mexican heritage. *1491* is an epic illustration of the history, landscape, and culture of the Americas prior to the Spanish conquest. Although I felt newly illuminated, I was still left with an intense yearning for the precise details of what these human beings were cooking and eating.

Questioning the mechanics of the modern world and getting too existential about supper can sometimes have dire consequences on the human psyche. Fortunately for me, this time it led not to a crisis but to another epiphany, through my introduction to the second love of my life after Virginia. Her name was Sophie D. Coe. Although she left this world as I was entering high school, she left behind, as a small part of her legacy, her book, *America's First Cuisines*. Through scholarly research, slightly cantankerous judiciousness, and just about the right amount of nerdiness, she wrote the only book that I currently know of that describes what the food of the Americas was before Spanish contact, and it's all based on fact. I had yet to learn that some of the basic foodstuffs that are not only taken for granted now, but that actually define the cuisine of other civilizations, originated in the Americas: potatoes, beans, chiles, tomatoes, avocados, squash, to name a few of the most important.

After reading *America's First Cuisines* multiple times, I realized that the final line in her book is the most important:

> "This book started with the promise that it was going
> to recount and celebrate the contribution of the
> New World, its lands and its peoples, to the cuisine of
> the world. It is to be hoped that it is not an overly
> Europe-centered account of the food of the Aztecs,
> the Maya, and the Inca and what happened to it
> during the first few decades of their coexistence with
> a fourth tribe, the Europeans. It should show us that
> not everybody eats the way we do, and that other
> culinary cultures can provide us not only with actual
> things to eat, but with food for thought as well. As well
> as enriching our diet, this encounter could also
> enrich our minds, and let us hope that this enrich-
> ment is but a beginning!"

Indeed this was just the beginning of my fascination with and study of the indigenous foodways of Occupied Northern Mexico, as I like to call it. The significance of Sophie D. Coe's quote, which is a fine punctuation to an incredible body of work, is that it illustrates that the transgressions and genocides of the past cannot be remediated, whitewashed, or changed.

Virginia and I endeavored to learn about a culture and history that had nearly been erased or mostly forgotten, and our intent was to try to carry the traditions and learned knowledge from well over 10,000 years of human perseverance into the future. We also fully understood that this was just a starting point in a lifetime of continual learning.

In addition to Ms. Coe's text, we built a whole library of books that have been carefully curated and studied, and brought on a botanist named Jeff Keeling, who is relentlessly peppered with questions and always produces answers mostly on the spot. Virginia also opened up my mind by nonchalantly pointing out native flowers and trees or by telling a story about making bread from mesquite beans in Terlingua, and getting "high" from not only the sweet fragrance but the ensuing rush from these nutrient-rich desert plants. She would recount making prickly pear wine with her friend and mentor Jonny Sufficool, and little did I know that I would wind up making that wine as well. This led to more questions and more research. She would also politely tell me,

> "Please, shut the fuck up."

if I was talking out of turn—which is invaluable from a comrade and a guiding force when you're on a sort of journalistic quest, or are in a situation and are not clear on what precisely you are doing.

The actual galvanizing part for me personally is not just visiting different points in Mexico and connecting the dots through information from books, but also witnessing firsthand how one of the most incredible human beings on the planet conducts life on a daily basis. Through my reading and Virginia's diligent research, I became fascinated by a Mexican (Zapotec) chef who uses indigenous ingredients and ancient techniques, like pureeing everything on a series of metates, to create dishes that she can honestly label as "prehispanico." We are fortunate to be able to visit her once or twice a year. Abigail Mendoza Ruiz is not only the chef-owner of Tlamanalli restaurant in Teotitlán del Valle, Oaxaca, Mexico, but also an obvious expert at whatever she puts her mind to. She appears to be the matriarch of her family, is in fact the Minister of Culture for the town and region, and—I believe—is the connection to thousands of years of indigenous culture. Also, this lady can cook. One of the most inspirational things I have ever tasted would be the *shnis shish*, or *agua de chepil con calabacitas tiernas*, or "weed water with tender squashes" (the translations from Zapotec to Spanish to English, which are from her book, make me laugh). It is a soup with squash flowers and tender native herbs of her region, and is one of her signature dishes. This inspired a lot of the subtle nuances in our cooking and especially our Squash Vine Soup with Chochoyotes, which is completely different than hers but definitely a nod of respect.

Here in Marfa, the landscape is beautiful and the weather mostly agreeable while unforgiving at times. Setting out to open our roadside saloon/mercantile, we tried to take everything into consideration with the understanding that you cannot be in control of everything at all times. We enlisted machines to help us do the work and learned to fix them on a daily basis. We constantly strive to learn about our environment, teach others, and learn from others. We welcome all visitors and if we don't have what you are looking for, we can offer a suggestion or a point in the right direction. We have forged relationships with guests and employees, in effect becoming friends, family, and community.

Our fundamental aim at the Capri is about respect and purity of intention. We want to utilize the original building, showcasing the simple and sturdy craftsmanship that makes it what it is. We inject our own stylistic identity, paying close attention to our fellow citizens of the Americas, our community, and visitors alike. We want to find edible plants and uncover techniques that might have been forgotten or not yet discovered. This book offers snapshots of the creation of the Capri, and some documentation of the first three years, but I feel like we have only just begun.

With consideration of all the variables in the world that all humans deal with, we are constantly striving to remember our initial points of inspiration and keep our purity of intention intact. We try to take the local economy and politics into account while taking into consideration those who came before us and especially the ones who will come after. Collaboration and social responsibility are crucial in a small town on a manmade border—and we all gotta eat.

Tortillas and Breads

The tortilla can be your napkin and your spoon at the same time. You can hide your tears in it as you comfort yourself in its warm, steamy skin. You can wing a dry stale tortilla at a friend or loved one that you feel has wronged you.

Nixtamal/Masa

NIXTAMALIZATION IS THE PROCESS OF cooking corn in an alkaline solution that softens and removes the tough outer coating and causes a chemical reaction on the interior. This chemical reaction makes the corn more nutritionally bioavailable and gives the corn the ability to be formed into a dough. To make the alkaline solution you use calcium chloride—also known as pickling salt, or *cal* in Spanish. "Nixtamalization" is really a back-formation or Anglicization of the Spanish word *nixtamal*, which is synonymous to "masa." Out of respect for the process, we call this *nixtamal*.

When we first started making *nixtamal*, even though I had tried-and-true recipes and had even made it multiple times with ladies in Mexico, I could never get it quite right. I stopped by to see my friend Jason who is the chef of all the Tacombi restaurants in New York. He was showing me their tortilla-making operation and I saw a piece of paper taped to the side of a giant stockpot. It said:

Tacombi
100 lb Maiz
1 lb Cal
80 Min Exacto!

For whatever reason, the *nixtamal* process finally clicked or gelled in my head. We scaled down the Tacombi version to a more manageable, gringo-sized recipe (the Tacombi recipe makes 150 pounds/68 kg masa, which is way to much to handle) because we don't have industrial machines to grind large batches of corn—just our good old hand grinder and metate.

When I refer to making *nixtamal* with "ladies" it is for a very specific reason. I mentioned that as I became interested in cooking I was not allowed to cook in the home because men don't cook in Mexico—except in one small village by the river where they make a hot rock soup as an offering to their wives, or in machismo-drenched chef ego-driven restaurants in the cities. Saying "home cooks" or "ladies" is a redundancy, because in the home the ladies are the only ones cooking, be it your sister, wife, mother, abuela, tia or any of the aforementioned family members of your friends or hosts. It was the ladies of Mexico—and only the ladies—who first introduced me to *nixtamalization* and I feel that recognizing that with a gender-specific noun is about the leanest nod of respect that I could give.

For a more thorough primer on *nixtamal* or the value of corn as a staple of the New World, you should read my favorite book, *America's First Cuisines*, by Sophie D. Coe.

Makes 2 pounds (90 g) masa

2 cups (340g)	dried non-GMO dent corn (we use Red Olotillo, Hopi Blue, Oaxacan Green, and Bloody Butcher varieties to name a few)
2 tbsp	cal

In a 6-quart (6-liter) nonreactive pot, combine the corn and 6 cups (1.4 liters) water and bring to a boil. Reduce to a simmer and stir in the *cal*. Allow to barely simmer for exactly 1 hour 20 minutes. Remove from the heat and let sit in the water for 12 hours or overnight.

Rinse the corn with fresh water, rubbing the kernels between your hands to remove the pericarp (the skin or hull).

Coarsely grind the corn once in a cast-iron Estrella or Victoria grain grinder. From there we process the masa to the desired consistency on our antique metate. For our soft masa recipe or tamales, we leave it coarser. For tortillas, the finer the masa is ground the better.

Tortillas

THERE IS NOT A SMELL that I find more seductive and comforting than fresh tortillas warming on a wood-fired comal. On my first trips to Mexico, I learned that the tortilla has much more of a role in our lives than just the multiple iterations of a staple food. The tortilla can be your napkin and your spoon at the same time. You can hide your tears in it as you comfort yourself in its warm, steamy skin. You can wing a dry stale tortilla at a friend or loved one that you feel has wronged you. You can even lure animals in with the tortilla, be they domesticated or wild, for whatever your purpose might require.

With this sort of reverence for the tortilla and the masa it is made from we tread lightly when it comes to adulteration. We make tortillas from native corn, *nixtamalize* it according to tradition, and grind it by hand. First, we assess the corn, its color, and flavor characteristics. Then if we want to add something to the masa, it is preferable that the addition be native as well, but above all harmonious and complementary.

We never set out to simply dye the tortillas for aesthetic effec; it is an ongoing experiment but not one that we began blindly, without culinary purpose, or ethnohistorical respect. Southern Mexico is the home of all of our gracious teachers who have taught us so much about the wide spectrum of color, flavor, and spirit that exists in the natural world, and that is so simply exemplified by an understanding of pH balance and an innate acumen for creating beauty. These are the humans that with a pomegranate, a slice of lime, and a pinch of ashes from the fire can show you every expression and hue—from transparent yellow to the purple drops of blood from the last dying dinosaur—in whatever saturation desired.

They are the wool-dyers and weavers from Teotitlán del Valle, the hand-carvers and painters of the Alebrijes in San Martín Tilcajete, and the assorted artisans of Chiapas. The shamans and brujos in San Juan Chamula, and those sweet children in the Lacandon jungle walking home from school with jaguars and shaking me down, trading expert beaded handicrafts for not enough pesos. The least we could do is honor them and make a green tortilla or two.

There are many options for keeping tortillas warm, from plastic tortilla warmers to ceramic dishes with lids to traditional Mexican baskets. We have hand-sewn warmers from the Tarahumara. They are made and sold by young ladies in Chihuahua City, and each one is slightly different in material and design. They are beautiful, and we like to support the indigenous peoples by buying their crafts. I think the most insulative are the weird cheap ones with printed chile peppers or the Virgin Mary on them. But all you really need is a sturdy tea towel, because the only thing that keeps tortillas warm is piling on more tortillas.

TORTILLA MASA (NATURAL NIXTAMAL)

Makes 10–12 tortillas
11 pounds (500 g) masa (see page 160)

These are tortillas we have made from corn that is nixtamalized, but au naturel, with no outside coloring or flavoring are completely dependent on being themselves.

Make the nixtamal as described in the recipe using one of these types of corn: Oaxacan Green, yellow dent, Bloody Butcher, Hopi Blue, White Olotillo. Run it through the grinder as directed. At this point, you can grind the masa to the consistency needed for tortillas on a metate (or you can tighten the grinding mechanism on the hand grinder and run it through a second time) and use them as is, or incorporate a powdered or juice-based flavoring or dye (see the recipes that follow).

TORTILLAS WITH POWDERS

Makes 10–12 tortillas
11 pounds (500 g) masa (see page 160)

Pick one:
50 g beet powder
35 g ground turmeric
40 g cacao powder
20 g Mesquite Powder (page 203)
80 g activated charcoal powder
40 g spirulina powder (Blue Majik)
35 g espresso powder

TORTILLAS WITH JUICES, HERBS, FLOWERS, LEAVES, AND BEYOND

Makes 10–12 tortillas
11 pounds (500 g) masa (see page 160)

Pick one:
Nasturtium flowers, whole
Nasturtium leaves, whole
Prickly pear juice
Epazote leaves, whole
Epazote leaves, chopped
Epazote leaf juice
Marigold petals, fresh
Marigold petals, dried

The amounts of powder to be used are not only dependent on the flavor of the *nixtamalized* corn, but also the taste and hue desired by the person making the masa and what other ingredients it will be paired with. After the masa is ground to your desired consistency, simply knead in the powder to evenly distribute.

Then there are the juices, chopped herbs, and flower petals that are much more subjective and open the gates of ultimate freedom and allow a person to be as calculated or arbitrary as they want in their tortilla making. Their masa, their choice. There is no limit to what can be done with this, but the most important detail cannot be forgotten: the final product has to taste good and be tortillas. After the masa is ground to your desired consistency, simply knead in the powder to evenly distribute.

SHAPE AND COOK THE TORTILLAS:

Once we have waded through that whole mess, it is time to cook the tortillas:

Preheat a comal or frying pan. It needs to be hot and it is nice to have two zones of heat, one that is really hot, and one even hotter.

Roll the masa into balls that are slightly smaller than a golf ball. Press them in a tortilla press of your choosing. We have multiple types but always defer to the cast-iron Victoria model.

Add a fresh pressed tortilla to the heated pan and cook on one side for a minute or two. Flip it over and cook on the second side for 1 minute. Then flip the tortilla back onto the first side over a direct flame or a separate pan heated on high until it puffs up like a balloon.

Serve immediately or store in a tortilla warmer.

Mesquite-Dusted Sourdough Bread with Ember-Scented Olive Oil

WE MAKE BREAD FROM OUR own sourdough starter and mesquite beans from particular trees around the Capri that we grind into flour. The mesquite beans lend an indescribable scent and flavor and are very nutritionally dense. I was originally inspired to do this by a story Virginia told me, about how she and her friend made mesquite bread in Terlingua one day and felt like they were on a "nutritional high" after eating it. We made a series of experiments using baker and cookbook author Jim Lahey's no-knead bread ratios and baking techniques for a very hydrated dough, hybridized with more traditional techniques and using our sourdough starter and our mesquite. We get our flour freshly milled from Barton Springs Mill in Austin. We use different ratios of Sonoran, Red Fife, and Yecora Rojo, which means we have to adjust our water ratios as we learn the nuances of each wheat. This is our base recipe, and although we use different flours, a person could even substitute all-purpose (plain) flour and it would still turn out great. This recipe can be divided in half, shortening the baking times to 20 minutes and 10 minutes respectively.

Makes 1 loaf

6 cups (800 g)	bread flour (strong white flour)
4½ tbsp (40 g)	mesquite flour, plus more for dusting
2 cups minus 1½ tbs (450 g)	water
150 g	sourdough starter (optional; if you don't have your own sourdough starter, substitute 150 g water)
2½ tsp (16 g)	salt
1¼ tsp (4 g)	active dry yeast
	Ember-Scented Olive Oil (page 205), for dipping

In a stand mixer fitted with a dough hook, combine the flours, water, sourdough starter, salt, and yeast. Process until the dough forms a smooth elastic ball, 6–7 minutes. (Alternatively, you can knead by hand for about 10 minutes.)

Transfer the dough to a lightly oiled bowl and cover with plastic wrap (cling film). Let rise at room temperature for 2 hours.

Preheat the oven to 450°F (230°C/Gas Mark 8) with a large Dutch oven (casserole) with a lid on inside.

Punch the dough and shape into a round. Return to the bowl and lightly dust the top with mesquite flour. Let rise again for 15 minutes.

Pour the dough in one quick motion into the preheated Dutch oven (casserole). Score the top of the dough with a lame (dough-slashing razor) or sharp knife and replace the lid. Bake for 30 minutes. Uncover and bake for an additional 15 minutes. Remove the bread from the pot and place on a rack to cool.

Serve with ember-scented olive oil for dipping.

Mesquite-Dusted Whole Wheat Bread with Ember-Scented Olive Oil

THIS BREAD RECIPE IS A slight variation on our sourdough bread, substituting whole wheat flour for 25 percent of the bread flour. We also sometimes use rye flour instead of the whole wheat. This base recipe is fun to experiment with. It can be divided in half, shortening the baking times to 20 minutes and 10 minutes respectively.

Makes 1 loaf

4 cups plus 7 tbsp (600 g)	bread flour (strong white flour)
1⅔ cups (200 g)	whole wheat (wholemeal) flour
4 ½ tbsp (40 g)	mesquite flour, plus more for dusting
2 cups minus 1½ tbsp (450 g)	water
150 g	sourdough starter (optional; if you don't have your own sourdough starter, substitute 150 g water)
1½ tsp (16 g)	salt
1¼ (4 g)	active dry yeast
	Ember-Scented Olive Oil (page 205), for dipping

In a stand mixer fitted with a dough hook, combine the flours, water, sourdough starter, salt, and yeast. Process until the dough forms a smooth elastic ball, 6–7 minutes. (Alternatively, you can knead by hand for about 10 minutes.)

Transfer the dough to a lightly oiled bowl and cover with plastic wrap (cling film). Let rise at room temperature for 2 hours.

Preheat the oven to 450°F (230°C/Gas Mark 8) with a large Dutch oven (casserole) with a lid on inside.

Punch the dough and shape into a round. Return to the bowl and lightly dust the top with mesquite flour. Let rise again for 15 minutes.

Pour the dough in one quick motion into the preheated Dutch oven (casserole). Score the top of the dough with a lame (dough-slashing razor) or sharp knife and replace the lid. Bake for 30 minutes. Uncover and bake for an additional 15 minutes. Remove the bread and place on a rack to cool.

Serve with ember-scented olive oil for dipping.

Mesquite Toast

THESE THIN SLICES OF TOAST are the perfect accompaniement for our Rabbit Liver Mousse (page 86). If you have leftover Mesquite-Dusted Bread I also highly encourage this use for it as a replacement for any cracker you might be using as a vehicle for cheese or other snacks.

Makes about 36 slices

½ loaf	Mesquite-Dusted Sourdough Bread (page 166)
½ loaf	Mesquite-Dusted Whole Wheat Bread (opposite)
½ cup (120 ml)	Ember-Scented Olive Oil (page 205)
	Kosher (flaked) salt

Preheat the oven to 350°F (180°C/Gas Mark 4).

Line sheet pans with parchment paper. Cut the bread into slices ¼-inch (6 mm) thick and lay the slices in single layers on the sheet pans. Brush lightly with the ember oil and place in the oven until golden and crisp, 5–6 minutes. Season lightly with salt.

Helados

We think about food and culinary endeavors as magical
art forms; ones that can take you far beyond the basic
need for sustenance.

Mesquite Bean Ice Cream

OUR MESQUITE BEAN ICE CREAM is one of the dishes that we are most proud of, one of the most popular items on the menu, one of the most mystifying dishes to our guests, and quite possibly the simplest thing to make.

Serves 6

7 ounces (200 g)	egg yolks (about 12)
2 cups (500 g)	half-and-half (single cream)
¾ cup plus 2 tbsp (170 g)	sugar
1½ tsp (4 g)	Diamond Crystal kosher (flaked) salt
50 g	mesquite powder, store-bought or homemade (page 203), plus more for serving
2	vanilla beans, split lengthwise
4 tsp (4 g)	Stabiwise (stabilizer)

In a blender, combine the egg yolks, half-and-half (single cream), sugar, salt, and mesquite powder and blend. Scrape in the vanilla seeds, reserving the pods.

Set a sous vide immersion circulator to 82.7°C. Add 1 vanilla pod to each of 2 vacuum-seal bags. Divide the ice cream base between the bags. Vacuum-seal the bags and place in the circulator bath for 45 minutes.

Chill in an ice bath until cool. Pour the base from the bags through a fine-mesh sieve, discard the vanilla pods, and whisk in the Stabiwise. Process the mixture in an ice-cream maker or divide into Pacojet beakers and freeze overnight.

Pacotize, if needed, and serve on a frozen plate dusted with mesquite powder.

Chocolate Ice Cream

UNDERSTANDING THE IMPORTANCE OF CACAO to the Americas and the world, we set out to make the simplest and purest-tasting chocolate ice cream. One key to the flavor of this ice cream is using couverture, a type of chocolate with a relatively high percentage of cocoa butter. We like to serve this on a frozen *barro negro* (the black pottery made in Oaxaca) plate with a dusting of Mexican cinnamon and chile or sometimes in a dried cacao pod on a bed of dried epazote and cinnamon sticks doused with mezcal and set alight for fragrance and theatrics.

Serves 6

2 cups plus 2 tbsp (500 ml)	organic whole milk
1 cup plus 1 tbsp (250 ml)	organic half-and-half (single cream)
¾ tsp (2 g)	kosher (flaked) salt
20 oz (560 g)	semisweet (64% cacao) chocolate wafers, preferably couverture
3 tsp (3 g)	Stabiwise (stabilizer)

In a 6-quart (6-liter) saucepot, scald the milk and half-and-half (single cream), then remove from the heat. Add the salt, then add the chocolate slowly while whisking to emulsify.

Add the Stabiwise and blend with a hand mixer. Strain through a chinois or fine-mesh sieve. Process the mixture in an ice-cream maker or divide into Pacojet beakers and freeze overnight.

Pacotize, if needed, and serve.

Strawberry, Mulberry, Agarita, and Poppy Sorbet

THIS IS A SORBET THAT we make in the late spring because the strawberries, mulberries, agaritas, and opium poppies come in all at the same time. Agaritas are native shrubs that grow in our area and by midsummer are loaded with tart red berries similar to currants. We don't get very much of each individual ingredient, so we mix them all together.

Serves 6

10 oz (300 g)	strawberries
10 oz (300 g)	mulberries
3 ½ oz (100 g)	agarita berries
3 ½ oz (100 g)	opium poppy pods
½ cup (100 g)	sugar
2 tbsp plus 1 tsp (50 g)	glucose
3 tbsp plus 1 tsp (50 g)	fresh lemon juice
3 tsp (4 g)	Stabiwise (stabilizer)

In a large saucepan, combine the strawberries, mulberries, agarita berries, poppy pods, sugar, glucose, lemon juice, Stabiwise, and ⅔ cup (150 g) water. Bring to a simmer for 10 minutes and then turn off the heat and allow to cool to room temperature.

Transfer the mixture to a high-powered blender and blend until smooth. Process the mixture in an ice-cream maker or divide into Pacojet beakers and freeze overnight.

Pacotize, if needed, and serve.

Key Lime Pie Sorbet

TINY LIMES ARE UBIQUITOUS IN Mexico and are served with just about everything. We call them Key limes in the States. We started out making a Key lime paleta with half-and-half, and then decided to lighten it up and make a sorbet out of it by replacing the half-and-half with yogurt. This gave the necessary acid and tang, and created a softer texture. I sometimes fantasize about serving this on graham cracker crumbs, but have yet to do it.

Serves 6s

1¾ cups (14 oz/395 g)	organic whole-milk yogurt
14 oz (400 ml)	simple syrup (1:1 ratio of sugar to water)
2 tbsp	grated lime zest
1½ cups (355 ml)	fresh Key lime juice
½ tsp	kosher (flaked) salt
2 tbsp	mesquite powder, store-bought or homemade (page 203), for dusting

In a blender, combine the yogurt, simple syrup, lime zest, lime juice, and salt. Blend until smooth. Process the mixture in an ice-cream maker or divide into Pacojet beakers and freeze overnight.

Pacotize, if needed, and serve in frozen bowls dusted with mesquite powder.

Durazno Blanco Raicilla Sorbet (White Peach with Mezcal)

BECAUSE OF THE EVERCHANGING AND dynamic weather patterns in Marfa, like early freezes and high winds, the fruit trees are never guaranteed to produce year to year. For example we were able to have white peaches from a single tree once in the last seven years. We had also just gotten in a line of raicillas from La Venenosa for the first time. For an appropriate texture in sorbets, it is sometimes necessary to add a little bit of alcohol. Generally a neutral spirit like vodka is used, but tasting the little brother of mezcals, raicilla, at the same time as the peaches were finally coming in, it only made sense to use the old spirit from Jalisco as a flavoring as well. (A fun thing you can do if you really want to nerd out is look up the history of raicilla.) To play this up, we like to serve the sorbet accompanied by a tiny shot of raicilla on the side.

Serves 6

4 lb 6 oz (2 kg)	white peaches, halved and pitted, skins on
2 cups (400 g)	granulated sugar
¾ cup (150 g)	invert sugar
3 tbsp plus 1 tsp (50 ml)	La Venenosa Raicilla Sur de Jalisco mezcal
2 tbsp plus 1 tsp (50 g)	glucose
2 tbsp (6 g)	Stabiwise (stabilizer)

In a high-powered blender, blend the peaches, granulated sugar, invert sugar, mezcal, glucose, and Stabiwise until smooth. Process the mixture in an ice-cream maker or divide into Pacojet beakers and freeze overnight.

Pacotize, if needed, and serve.

Prickly Pear Rose Sorbet

WHENEVER THE SEASON IS RIGHT, Jonny Sufficool and I pick tons of prickly pears to make wine from. We put a little bit of the fresh juice aside for drinking and making sorbet. Drinking about ½ cup (120 ml) a day is extremely nutrtious. Drink too much and you will hallucinate.

Serves 6

3 ½ oz (100 g)	red rose petals
½ cup (100 g)	sugar
4 cups (850 g)	prickly pear juice
7 tbsp (150 g)	glucose
2 tbsp plus 2 tsp (40 ml)	organic rose water
2 tbsp (30 ml)	vodka
2 tbsp (6 g)	Stabiwise
	Rose Petal Sugar (recipe follows), for serving

Place the rose petals in a heatproof bowl. In a saucepan, combine the sugar and a scant 1 cup (200 g) water and bring to a simmer. Remove from the heat and pour over the rose petals. Steep for 10–15 minutes. Strain through a chinois or fine-mesh sieve and cool.

In a blender, combine the rose petal syrup, prickly pear juice, glucose, rose water, vodka, and Stabiwise and blend until smooth. Process the mixture in an ice-cream maker or divide into Pacojet beakers and freeze overnight.

Pacotize, if needed, and serve with rose petal sugar.

ROSE PETAL SUGAR
Makes 3½ oz (100 g)

1 ¾ oz (50 g)	red rose petals
¼ cup (50 g)	sugar

In a spice grinder or with a mortar and pestle, grind the rose petals and sugar together. Sift through a fine-mesh sieve and store in an airtight container.

Whole Roasted Pineapple/Smoky Pineapple Sorbet

WE LIKE TO ROAST PINEAPPLES whole in the BBQ. It concentrates the sweetness and gives a slight hint of smoke that translates well to the sorbet form and lends a mysterious quality to the flavor. Once, as a joke course, we sent a whole roasted pineapple with four steak knives sticking out of it, a pile of chile limes, and some *sal de chapulín* to our friend and photographer of this book, Douglas Friedman. Everyone at his table loved it, and then the other tables in the dining room started ordering it, even though it was not on the menu. The pineapple is indeed quite tasty on its own. We usually do six at a time, but it can be any number as long as they are whole. To roast, light a fire in the BBQ using oak, pecan, or mesquite. Ventilate it so that you maintain a temperature around 300°F (150°C). Place your pineapples offset so they are smoking, not grilling, and roast for 3 hours.

Serves 6

1 lb (500 g)	roasted pineapple, peeled and chopped
7 ½ tbsp (150 g)	simple syrup (1:1 ratio of sugar to water)
2 tsp (10 g)	fresh lime juice
2 tsp (2 g)	Stabiwise

In a high-powered blender, combine the pineapple, simple syrup, lime juice, and Stabiwise and blend until smooth. Process the mixture in an ice-cream maker or divide into Pacojet beakers and freeze overnight.

Pacotize, if needed, and serve.

Jamaica (Hibiscus) Paletas

ONE OF THE MOST POPULAR and refreshing drinks in Mexico is *agua fresca de Jamaica,* lightly sweetened hibiscus tea over ice. We decided to make a more concentrated version to turn into an ice-cold refreshing *paleta.*

Makes 12 paletas

3½ cups (700 g)	sugar
1	Mexican cinnamon stick
3 cups (130 g)	dried hibiscus flowers
½ cup (120 ml)	fresh lime juice
2 tsp (2 g)	Stabiwise (stabilizer)

If using a metal *paleta* or ice pop (lolly) mold, place in the freezer and let chill for 1–2 hours.

In a saucepan, combine 9 cups (2.13 liters) water, the sugar, and cinnamon stick and bring to a simmer. Remove from the heat and add the hibiscus flowers. Let steep for 20 minutes. Strain through a chinois or fine-mesh sieve and cool.

In a blender, combine the hibiscus syrup, lime juice, and Stabiwise and blend until smooth.

Pour the *paleta* mixture into the frozen *paleta* mold. Insert the sticks and freeze overnight.

At the restaurant we submerge the mold in a bath of tap-temperature water for 5–10 seconds, then quickly remove the pops and transfer them to a prefrozen sheet pan lined with parchment paper. Store in the freezer until serving. This allows for quick service at the end of the meal even when hosting a few guests at your home. It is also advantageous because it allows the *paletas,* slightly warmed during the unmolding process, to refreeze and retain their shape.

Tamarindo con Chapulines Paletas

A LOT OF THE CANDY in Mexico is made with tamarind paste and spicy chile, and I love it. My favorite is called Pelon Pelo Rico! We like to make these tamarind ice pops and dip them into a spicy salt mix made with grasshoppers. It is also nice to chase it with a little mezcal.

Makes 12 paletas

1¼ cups (250 g)	sugar
1⅓ cups (250 g)	piloncillo or granulated sugar
2½ cups (500 g)	tamarind concentrate
2 tsp (2 g)	Stabiwise (stabilizer)
1¾ tsp (5 g)	kosher (flaked) salt
2 tbsp (10 g)	dried pequín chiles
1½ oz (40 g)	chapulines (dried grasshoppers)

If using a metal *paleta* or ice pop (lolly) mold, place in the freezer and let chill for 1–2 hours.

In a saucepan, combine 1⅔ cups (400 ml) water and both sugars and bring to a simmer. Remove from the heat, strain through a chinois or fine-mesh sieve, and cool.

In a blender, combine the sugar syrup, tamarind concentrate, and Stabiwise. Blend until smooth.

Pour the *paleta* mixture into the frozen *paleta* mold. Insert the sticks and freeze overnight.

To unmold, submerge the mold in a bath of tap-temperature water for 5–10 seconds and then quickly remove the *paletas,* transferring them to a prefrozen sheet pan lined with parchment paper. Store in the freezer until serving.

Combine the salt, chiles, and *chapulines* in a molcajete or mortar and pestle and grind into a coarse powder. Serve with the *paletas.*

Apricot-Chamomile Paletas

THROUGHOUT OUR RESEARCH IN BOOKS and in the field, we have come across the combination of apricots and chamomile flowers a few times. In books it is intriguing, but in person it tastes so good it feels a little naughty. Fortunately for us, when the weather acts right, we get more apricots from our tiny orchard than we can handle. We force them through a litany of iterations that the fortunate never have to suffer. In terms of joy, this *paleta* is second place only to standing under the tree and gorging yourself on the warm sun-ripened fruit itself. If you can't find loose dried chamomile flowers, feel free to use chamomile tea, but check the box to be sure there aren't other herbs or spices in there.

Makes 12 paletas

1½ cups (150 g)	sugar
1½ cups (60 g)	organic chamomile flowers, dried, or 8 bags organic chamomile tea
2 lb (910 g)	ripe apricots, peeled and pitted
¼ cup (60 ml)	fresh lime juice

If using a metal *paleta* or ice pop (lolly) mold, place in the freezer and let chill for 1–2 hours.

In a saucepan, combine 4 cups (950 ml) water, the sugar, and chamomile flowers and bring to a simmer for 10 minutes. Remove from the heat and allow to cool. Strain through a chinois or fine-mesh sieve and return to the saucepan.

Add the apricots to the chamomile syrup and simmer for 20 minutes. Allow to cool and push through a tamis or fine-mesh sieve. Add the lime juice. Refrigerate until well chilled.

Pour the apricot mixture into the frozen *paleta* mold. Insert the sticks and freeze overnight.

To unmold, submerge the mold in a bath of tap-temperature water for 5–10 seconds and then quickly remove the *paletas*, transferring them to a prefrozen sheet pan lined with parchment paper. Store in the freezer until serving.

Cucumber, Mexican Elderflower, and Tequila Paletas

THIS *PALETA* IS A REFRESHING and unique taste of the Capri in the compact and delicious form of an ice pop. The Mexican elders bloom all over the property, the cucumbers grow in the garden, and the bar is always stocked with my favorite tequila. If you don't have access to fresh elderflowers, you can substitute store-bought elder syrup or ½ cup (120 ml) St-Germain elderflower liqueur.

Makes 12 paletas

4 lb (1.8 kg)	Armenian or English (seedless) cucumbers, peeled, seeded, and roughly chopped
6 tbsp	fresh lemon juice
1 cup (240 ml)	Mexican Elderflower Syrup (recipe follows)
½ cup (120 ml)	Corralejo Reposado tequila
2 tsp (2 g)	Stabiwise (stabilizer)

If using a metal *paleta* or ice pop (lolly) mold, place in the freezer and let chill for 1–2 hours.

In a high-powered blender, combine the cucumbers, lemon juice, elderflower syrup, tequila, and Stabiwise and blend until smooth.

Pour the *paleta* mixture into the frozen *paleta* mold. Insert the sticks and freeze overnight.

To unmold, submerge the mold in a bath of tap-temperature water for 5–10 seconds, then quickly remove the *paletas* and transfer them to a prefrozen sheet pan lined with parchment paper. Store in the freezer until serving.

MEXICAN ELDERFLOWER SYRUP
Makes 3 cups (750 ml)

2 cups (50 g)	freshly picked Mexican elderflowers
2 cups (400 g)	sugar

Place the elderflowers in a large heatproof bowl. In a large saucepan, combine 2 quarts (2 liters) water and the sugar and bring to a simmer. Remove from the heat and pour over the elderflowers. Let steep for 10–15 minutes. Strain through a chinois or fine-mesh sieve and cool. Store in the refrigerator for up to 2 weeks.

No Es Cafe Paletas

THIS *PALETA* IS INSPIRED BY our friend Johannes, who is from Tulum, Mexico. He was twenty years old before he saw real coffee. At the time, all they had in his remote part of the Yucatán was Nescafé. All the locals referred to it as "No es café," which translates to "This is not coffee."

Makes 12 paletas

9 cups (2.13 liters)	organic whole milk
1 cup (45 g)	instant coffee granules
2¼ cups (450 g)	sugar
2 tsp	vanilla extract (preferably Mexican)
2 tbsp (6 g)	Stabiwise (stabilizer)

If using a metal *paleta* or ice pop (lolly) mold, place in the freezer and let chill for 1–2 hours.

In a large saucepan, combine the milk, instant coffee, sugar, vanilla, and Stabiwise and bring to a simmer. Remove from the heat, strain through a chinois or fine-mesh sieve, and cool.

Pour the *paleta* mixture into the frozen *paleta* mold. Insert the sticks and freeze overnight.

To unmold, submerge the mold in a bath of tap-temperature water for 5–10 seconds and then quickly remove the *paletas*, transferring them to a prefrozen sheet pan lined with parchment paper. Store in the freezer until serving.

Nopales Paletas

WE ADD A LITTLE PINEAPPLE to the cactus pads in this *paleta* both for sweetness and acidity. The short salt-curing of the cactus pads removes the slime and leaves a little residual salinity that brings out the unique and vegetal flavor.

Makes 12 paletas

2 lb (910 g)	nopales (cactus paddles), cleaned of spines, rinsed, and cut into medium dice
3 cups (400 g)	kosher (flaked) salt
1 cup (200 g)	sugar
¼ cup (65 g)	honey
½ cup (120 ml)	fresh lime juice
3 cups (500 g)	medium-diced fresh pineapple
3 tbsp (9 g)	Stabiwise (stabilizer)

If using a metal *paleta* or ice pop (lolly) mold, place in the freezer and let chill for 1–2 hours.

In a large nonreactive bowl, toss the nopales with the salt and let sit for at least 1 hour.

In a saucepan, combine 2 cups (475 ml) water, the sugar, and honey and bring to a simmer to dissolve. Remove from the heat and cool.

Thoroughly wash the nopales to remove the salt and slime and let drain in a colander.

In a high-powered blender, combine the nopales, lime juice, pineapple, honey syrup, and Stabiwise and blend until smooth.

Pour the mixture into the frozen *paleta* mold. Insert the sticks and freeze overnight.

To unmold, submerge the mold in a bath of tap-temperature water for 5–10 seconds and then quickly remove the *paletas*, transferring them to a prefrozen sheet pan lined with parchment paper. Store in the freezer until serving.

Sandia (Watermelon) Paletas

THIS IS ONE OF THE best—just pure, ripe watermelon frozen on a stick, perfect for dipping in tequila. Treat yourself!

Makes 12 paletas

2 cups (400 g)	sugar
20 cups (4.73 liters)	chopped seedless watermelon (from about 3 lb/1.4 kg fruit)
½ cup (120 ml)	fresh lime juice
1 tbsp (8 g)	kosher (flaked) salt
2 tsp (2 g)	Stabiwise (stabilizer)

If using a metal *paleta* or ice pop (lolly) mold, place in the freezer and let chill for 1–2 hours.

In a saucepan, combine 3 cups (710 ml) water and the sugar and bring to a simmer. Remove from the heat and cool.

In a high-powered blender, combine the syrup with the watermelon, lime juice, salt, and Stabiwise and blend until smooth.

Pour the *paleta* mix in to pre frozen *paleta* mold. Insert the sticks and freeze overnight.

To unmold, submerge the mold in a bath of tap-temperature water for 5–10 seconds and then quickly remove the *paletas*, transferring them to a prefrozen sheet pan lined with parchment paper. Store in the freezer until serving.

"Five Alive" Paletas

WHEN I WAS A KID, the closest thing to fruit juice my mother would buy was a fruit punch/citrus blend that came in a bright-blue carton and was called Five Alive. It's unclear how much actual juice was present in this beverage, but I loved it. I resurrected the old ghost from the 80s and put it in *paleta* form with a little Campari. None of the kids I work with have ever heard of Five Alive, so I seem to be the only one in on the joke—and now you are, too.

Makes 12 paletas

2 cups (400 g)	sugar
2	Mexican cinnamon sticks
2 cups (475 ml)	red grapefruit juice
2 cups (475 ml)	orange juice
1 cup (240 ml)	clementine juice
1 cup (240 ml)	fresh lemon juice
1 cup (240 ml)	fresh lime juice
½ cup (120 ml)	Campari
3 tsp (3 g)	Stabiwise (stabilizer)

If using a metal *paleta* or ice pop (lolly) mold, place in the freezer and let chill for 1–2 hours.

In a saucepan, combine 3 cups (710 ml) water, the sugar, and cinnamon sticks. Bring to a simmer. Remove from the heat and cool. Discard the cinnamon sticks.

In a pitcher (jug), combine the syrup, all the fruit juices, the Campari, and Stabiwise and blend with a hand blender. Strain through a chinois or fine-mesh sieve.

Pour the *paleta* mixture into the frozen *paleta* mold. Insert the sticks and freeze overnight.

To unmold, submerge the mold in a bath of tap-temperature water for 5–10 seconds and then quickly remove the *paletas*, transferring them to a prefrozen sheet pan lined with parchment paper. Store in the freezer until serving.

Entertaining, West Texas-Style

Here, entertaining with largesse is a ritual. We welcome our guests with lots of food, lots of drink, booming voices, laughter, and big open arms.

THE LONG ROAD HOME

by Virginia

I've had people call me a hostess in the past, although I've never thought of myself as a hostess. I just believe that sitting around a table sharing food and drink can ignite all kinds of wild experiences. Those moments can expand your view of the world, give you a moment to properly listen to someone; it can spark love of all different kinds, it can even change the course of your life. It doesn't matter if you are seated at a formal table, on the floor, around a fireplace, or around the back of a pickup truck. The potential for expansion exists in the pauses we take when we share food and libations.

Texans have a tendency toward ebullient and perhaps excessive styles of entertaining. As a historic ranching culture—in a state that is larger than the country of France, populated by ranches that ranged into the hundreds of thousands of acres—people traveled long distances to see one another, to be together. To do so, they traversed endless expanses of terrain without the benefit of modern infrastructure. Perhaps the big parties were a gesture of appreciation from the hosts to their guests for their Herculean efforts to visit. Whatever the reason, it is certainly the impulse to reward your guests for their lengthy travels that has created the mythology that everything is bigger in Texas.

In the movie *Giant*, which was filmed around Marfa in 1956, Elizabeth Taylor arrives at a West Texas ranch and is welcomed with a traditional barbacoa out in a sunbeaten and drought-ridden pasture. Full cows are cooked on expansive grills and in underground pits. The closest neighbors live fifty miles away, but they all have come out in their Sunday best to meet the illustrious newcomer from back East. The party has all of the qualities one would expect in Texas: cowboy boots, hats, lots and lots of meat, and a vast setting of endless horizons.

Here, entertaining with largesse is a ritual. We welcome our guests with lots of food, lots of drink, booming voices, laughter, and big open arms. This is as much the case in Marfa today as it was in the '50s. People still have to travel a long way to get here. We have to treat them with the respect that journey deserves. In Oaxaca, when you arrive at someone's home, they offer a small and delicate copita of mezcal to welcome you and honor your journey and visit. When you arrive at the Capri, we offer you an inappropriately large mezcal. And then another. That's Texas-style.

As I was growing up, my family habitually collected around the dinner table, and there were always artists, dancers, academics, musicians, politicians, historians, and rowdy friends from around the globe to be fed and entertained. I don't remember who was coming to dinner at the ranch on this specific night, but my mother suggested we go duck hunting at sunrise the next morning so she could serve proper wild duck for her guests. She is always keen to illustrate that the best food comes from the land and not the grocery store. There is a pond behind the house we call the "pajama pond." It's so close to the house all you have to do is roll out of bed, put on your rubber boots, and walk down for the first flight of birds as the sun comes up. When we got there, we both, yawning, leaned on opposite sides of the same oak tree weeping with Spanish moss. I was shooting one of my mother's old English Purdey shotguns. As the first ducks were flying in, I raised the gun to my shoulder. The trigger stuck. I couldn't pull off a shot. Whispering to my mother what was happening, she said,

"Trade guns with me."

As we passed the guns toward one another, the second flight glided in over the trees. She didn't have time to get the gun to her shoulder so she shot from the hip, literally. She shot a double. Two cartridges, two birds, from the hip. My only response was

"Alright, Annie Oakley, I'm going back to bed."

At dinner that night, I told the story to the awe of everyone around the table. It is hard to keep up with a Texas lady who entertains like that.

The entertaining experiences in Texas vary widely; like in most places, there are extremes on either end of the spectrum. I've been to a black-tie dinner where the guests were transported to the top of a mountain by helicopter. All of the host's family silver and china was transported by netted slings dangling from the bottom of the helicopter. It flew back and forth to deliver supplies to the highest point on the ranch. Then it flew the guests up to their dinner in the sky. Equally inspiring are the times I've sat on the banks of the Rio Grande, muddy, cold, and wet, to eat a cheese sandwich for dinner with ornithologists and botanists. I was enthralled with their lives—so attuned to minute details of existence, while my own life seemed like only broad sweeping brushstrokes, generalities in search of common ground.

The principles of Texas hospitality were top of mind when Fairfax and I started Ballroom. Hosting people is a constant for us now, but we learned the hard way through a plethora of mistakes what to do, how to do it, and when. In May of 2009 we hosted our first Ballroom benefit in Marfa on a ranch just west of town. April and May bring tumultuous weather to the high desert plains. Rains, dust storms, lightning storms, you name it and it will happen in those two months. The day we were preparing the benefactors' dinner for two hundred or so people, I called out to the ranch where we were hosting the event for an update on the setup. Our gallery manager at the time answered his phone.

"How are things going out there?"
"Well, we are putting out some fires," he said.
"Of course you are. We are hosting a dinner for two hundred."
"No, we are literally putting out fires!"

As lightning struck the ground on the ranch, the dry grasses would immediately ignite, over and over again. In 2012, we hosted our second benefit on the same ranch. Two hundred people out on the land, just seated for dinner, and out of the darkness with no warning arrived the most torrential downpour I might have ever seen. Guests rushed for cover, the dinner abruptly ended, and then spiraled into a tequila-drinking soiree of epic proportions. We don't host benefits out in the landscape in April or May anymore. It takes a while, but we finally learn. These disastrous attempts to defy the odds and entertain hundreds of people without the benefit of cover helped inspire the advent of the Capri as a restaurant, with bricks and mortar to help us control our environment, just a little.

But when the weather is kind, there are times we still like to load up the truck and take the Capri on the road. There is a place (let's keep the name of it a secret) we love to take people to give them a sense of where they are. So many people come in and out so quickly. If you never leave the town grid, if your tires never touch the gravel or your feet the dirt, it's difficult to understand the landscape and the geography of this place. The sun-downer spot in question is a potent vista looking across a canyon, over the Rio Grande and into the Sierra Madres of Mexico.

We pack up the back of the truck with the necessary amenities, mezcal mostly and some gorgeous food just in case. Once the pavement ends and the dirt road begins, you see the shift from desert plains to canyons that periodically pierce the flatlands along the Rio Grande. We pull off on the side of the road and pour some mezcal. Often people don't even realize how close we are to Mexico in Marfa. People tend to get real quiet when they stare off into this particular distance. There is a lot to ponder standing there.

We once had someone say,

"I fly eighteen hours to get to Africa to see this kind of landscape."

This land conjures the feeling you get from that kind of exotic, faraway landscape. It sparks the traveler mentality—the kind where you are learning something about the place and yourself. You are not just passing through or checking it off a list. Being out on the land, the ranches, the national park, the state park is the most important part of being here. It helps the rest make sense, pulls it all together.

That sense of place lends context to the artwork installed here. When you place Judd's work or even the work of younger artists in this broader cultural context of landscape and border, one can begin to understand the magnitude of this regional enclave. It is no longer a mystery why this island of high art exists in what people call the middle of nowhere. This same vista, this same experience, can provide a platform for understanding the food and historical culinary inspirations of the Capri as well.

The first night we opened the Capri, it was a soft opening, a very soft opening. We invited friends, and friends of friends, just by sending out messages over the text machine. It turned into a vibrant evening with loads more humans than we ever had expected. I was standing in the corner behind the bar watching to see how people felt and moved in the room. As my eyes scanned the room, they suddenly stopped on a scene that at once made me smile and produced a furrowed brow. I was watching Solange Knowles, not an unfamiliar figure in Marfa, speaking to a Buddhist nun in full regalia. I didn't know why that beautiful Buddhist nun was here, and I didn't even know whom to ask to remind me why. I was concerned I had not had enough sleep. Or perhaps someone had slipped Everclear into my margarita, those magical death potions from the '90s that I used to call PCP margaritas. But I turned into the plating room to ask Rocky to please confirm the sighting. He did. It was true. No PCP margarita had passed my lips. It's always wild and weird in Marfa, but even for here that seemed particularly inspiring and confusing. Later that night Sean Daly brought the nun to our cabinet of crystals in the tea room. She blessed the crystals and the Capri with good fortune and love.

We still try to focus on creating the backdrop for this kind of synchronicty to happen, both out in the landscape and in the restaurant. In the tea room, the small lounge off the Capri dining room, we moved in a piano to replace the idea of high tea. It is quite a rare and special piano with a long history and story of its own. When we opened Ballroom, my mother rescued the piano from storage and found a restorer to repair its old bones. We had never had a room big enough to house it permanently in Marfa. For years it sat in storage and was brought out only for special Ballroom concerts. It is a Steinway grand built in 1920 for Kathryn, my great-grandmother. When the restorer got his hands on it he noticed something was slightly amiss. The black lacquer was somehow out of place. He called my mother and asked permission to remove a small spot of the lacquer on the belly of the piano to see what was underneath. To his amazement, he was correct, the black lacquer was a later addition. Before its mysterious makeover, the original beauty was ribbon mahogany and one of only a few built of this precious wood in 1920 by Steinway.

Today, at the Capri, its current life entails magical moments when locals and visitors climb behind this beautiful beast and unleash its auditory glory with their talented fingers. I have sat by the fire in the bar on many nights since we moved the piano, thinking how incredible it is to witness people who I never knew played piano change the course of an evening. Pianos hold such a unique language. They were the after-dinner drawing room entertainment before radio and television, the formal language of music in historic concert halls, and the salacious call to dance of the proper old juke joints. It's incredible to watch its power to bring strangers together and change the shape of their hearts in that moment.

Not long ago we hosted one of my favorite events in the pergola laden with wild grapevines that sits in the garden. It was a Ballroom public program in conjunction with the group show "Hyperobjects." The artist and soil scientist Nance Klehm brought a plethora of soil samples from different local terrains as well as from her Midwestern home. There was composted soil, sandy desert soil, Ballroom soil, worked Capri garden soil, and so on. We were hosting a soil tasting to connect and understand the indelible nature and power of this most fundamental substance through the sense of taste. It was crazy and weird and totally invigorating. Attending were ranchers, ceramicists, naturalists, locals, and passersby. The gatherings that go deep and off-kilter are always the most exciting.

We have a small and unassuming artist-in-residency program at the Capri. If there is available space we want to fill it with artists, musicians, writers. This residency is separate from the Ballroom and does not require curatorial intervention or board approval. There is no application process. The artists who work at the Capri have come to us through the organic process of connections and introductions. It is a whimsical endeavor to engage people on a deeper level than just dinner in a restaurant. The artists work in the Capri space and inevitably end up sitting at the bar to engage in conversation with locals and visitors. They bring a layer of life and conversation to the space that might otherwise lie fallow. Art, music, and food are inextricable in this space. The residency has hosted the professional skateboarder and painter Brian Lotti; the performance artist and sculptor Lucian Shapiro; the weaver Matthias De Vogel from Amsterdam; and the Savannah, Georgia, painter-turned-Marfa resident Shea Slemmer, to name a few. These programs are both a gesture of our hospitality to the arts community, and a way of continuing to curate moments of inspiration and connection for anyone who comes through the Capri's doors.

I wish I had a portrait of every single person that has come through the Capri. Some leave immediately because we don't serve Bud Light. Some stay for hours and return every night. They arrive in private planes and RVs, on road trips in muddy cars filled with five dogs, in strikingly out-of-place Lamborghinis, on motorcycles and bicycles. They come from every continent on the globe. They are all in motion but they come through the door and they sit for a while.

Bases and
Sauces

This was just the beginning of my fascination with and study of the indigenous foodways of Occupied Northern Mexico, as I like to call it. The galvanizing part for me personally is not just visiting different points in Mexico and connecting the dots through information from books, but also from witnessing firsthand how some of the most incredible human beings on the planet conduct life on a daily basis.

Onion or Leek Top Ash

WHEN YOU TURN THE FRESH onion tops into ash, they still retain an onion scent with a more carbonized and complex flavor. We use this as a seasoning in our Peruvian potato dish (see page 94) to echo the flavors of the fresh onion in the crème fraîche and to add a layer of complexity.

Makes about 1 cup (240 ml)

10	leeks (or onion plants from the garden), green parts only

Preheat the oven to 400°F (200°C/Gas Mark 6).

Separate, wash, and spin the leek or onion tops in the salad spinner. Arrange the leaves in a single layer on sheet pans and roast until they are dry, fragrant, and blackened, about 2 hours.

Remove from the oven. Crumble the tops with your hands or in a food processor and then pass through a tamis or a fine-mesh sieve. Store in an airtight container with a silica packet until ready to use.

Sal de Chapulín

SAL DE GUSANO IS A traditional condiment in Mexico. A blend of salt, dried worms, and dried chile, we love using it in the bar for drinks, and also as a seasoning for foods in the kitchen. We don't always tell people that. Dried gusanos are virtually impossible to get in the US, but pre-mixed *sal de gusano* is readily available on the Internet. Unfortunately, these blends can be dubious and a little expensive. Here, instead, is a similar spicy salt, but made with *chapulines*, which are dried grasshoppers. My grandfather F.G. Barnette lives in North Carolina and grows a pile of chiles for me every year. We combine those with *chapulines* from Oaxaca to make our own special blend of *sal de chapulín*.

Makes 2 cups (480 ml)

1 cup (50 g)	chapulines (dried grasshoppers)
8–10	dried árbol chiles, depending on your taste for heat
1 cup (135 g)	kosher (flaked) salt

On a hot comal or in a dry frying pan, toast the *chapulines* until fragrant. Do the same for the chiles. Allow both to cool.

In a spice grinder or with a molcajete, combine the *chapulines* and the chiles with the salt and grind to your desired consistency. (We do it very fine for cocktail garnish or more on the coarse side if it is to be served with a steak.) Store in an airtight container.

Mesquite Powder

MESQUITE POWDER HAS BEEN QUITE the culinary epiphany for me. The flavor, smell, and nutritional value are unmatched by anything else. It is so distinct that we have it bookend a meal at the Capri starting with the bread in the beginning and the ice cream at the end. In far west Texas, mesquite trees are all over the place, invasive even. When we first started using mesquite we were told that in order to process enough we would need a diesel-powered hammer mill. We also learned that every tree produces pods with differing flavor characteristics. We developed a method for extracting the powder to supply our restaurant that requires no industrial equipment and the note in the ingredient list below referencing "your favorite tree" is an acknowledgment that each tree produces pods with different flavors. Mesquite powder of wonderful quality can also be ordered online very easily.

Makes about 1 quart (1 liter)

8 qt (8 liters)	mesquite pods from your favorite tree

Preheat a convection (fan-assisted) oven to 300°F (150°C). You can use a conventional oven at the same temperature or the blazing sun for 2–3 days if your climate allows.

Arrange the pods in a single layer on sheet pans and bake until they are dry and fragrant, about 20 minutes. Remove from the oven and allow the pods to cool.

Working in small batches, process the pods in a high-powered blender at full tilt to separate the outer shell from the bean and the actual pith in between, which becomes the powder. Then pass through a tamis or a fine-mesh sieve. Store in an airtight container with a silica packet until ready to use.

Fig Leaf Ash

TOASTED FIG LEAVES GIVE THE scent and flavor of toasted coconut, which we find interesting. We often coat fresh goat cheese with the ash and wrap it in a fig leaf for three days and then serve the cheese warm from the oven or heated with a kitchen torch. We also sneak the ash into some of our shrimp (prawn) dishes, which are served with smoldering fig leaves for garnish.

Makes 1 cup (240 ml)

40	fresh fig leaves, stems and large midribs removed

Preheat the oven to 400°F (200°C/Gas Mark 6).

Arrange the leaves in a single layer on sheet pans and roast until they are dry, fragrant, and starting to blacken, about 2 hours.

Remove from the oven. Crumble the leaves with your hands or in a food processor and then pass through a tamis or a fine-mesh sieve. Store in an airtight container with a silica packet until ready to use.

Achiote Paste

ACHIOTE IS A TRADITIONAL PASTE/marinade made by grinding up annatto seeds, which grow in the tropics, and mixing them with acidic citrus juices to make the paste. The paste is used to make the Yucatecan dish *cochinita pibil*: A baby pig is marinated with the paste, wrapped in banana leaves, and then slow-roasted in either an underground pit or an oven. Yucatecan recipes for the paste use the juice of bitter oranges, but elsewhere in the world we use sweet oranges, limes, lemons, or even vinegar to replicate this. The annatto adds a very distinctive taste and bright red color. You can buy premade achiote that does not have the dreaded red dye #40 but we prefer to make our own so as to control the flavors and adjust at our discretion. We use this to make our own version of *pibil* but in the form of duck confit.

Makes 1 cup (240 ml)

4 tbsp	annatto seeds
2 tsp	cumin seeds
2 tsp	coriander seeds
2 tsp	dried Mexican oregano
3	whole cloves
1	bay leaf
1 tsp	black peppercorns
1 tsp	Diamond Crystal kosher (flaked) salt
4	garlic cloves, peeled
1 tsp	grated lime zest
1 tsp	grated orange zest
2 tbsp	distilled white vinegar
2 tbsp	prickly pear vinegar

On a hot comal or in a dry frying pan, toast the annatto, cumin, coriander, oregano, cloves, and bay leaf until fragrant. In a food processor, combine the toasted spices, peppercorns, salt, garlic, lime zest, orange zest, and both vinegars and blend to make a smooth red paste. (Alternatively, mash together on a metate.) Store in an airtight container for up to 4 weeks.

Ember-Scented Olive Oil

I TOTALLY TOOK THIS IDEA from the Argentine chef Francis Mallmann. Virginia and I were having lunch at Il Buco, one of our favorite haunts/hideouts in New York City and there was a copy of his book *Mallmann on Fire* on the shelf next to me. I grabbed it and opened to the page of his ember oil. I thought this was a brilliant idea. For the Capri version, we use organic Texas or California extra virgin olive oil, chiles grown by my grandfather, and pequíns supplied by Virginia's mother.

Makes 3 quarts (3 liters)

3–5	pieces of mesquite wood (because some will burn away and you want the choicest charcoal-like piece), 4–6 inches (10–15 cm) in diameter, 2 feet (60 cm) long
3 qt (3 liters)	extra virgin olive oil, preferably organic from Texas or California
5	dried árbol chiles
5	dried cayenne or Tabasco chiles
15	dried pequín chiles

In a grill or fireplace, build a small fire with the mesquite wood and allow it to burn for 1–2 hours.

In a 6-quart stockpot, combine the oil and chiles, allowing 4 inches clearance at the top.

With tongs, choose a piece of the burning mesquite log that is around 8 inches (20 cm) long and is firm but still smoldering, carefully completely submerge it in the olive oil, and then release. Let everything steep for 1 day and up to 1 week. The oil keeps longer but should be strained after 1 week to avoid the flavor getting too strong.

If you are not going to use the ember oil within 1 week, strain it through a chinois or fine-mesh sieve and store in an airtight container.

Chiltomate

CHILTOMATE COMES FROM THE YUCATÁN region of Mexico and is considered to be the earliest tomato salsa that is cooked—though it is lovely served cold as well. It is slightly spicy because of the habaneros and has the consistency of a light, fresh marinara. We like to serve it with tempura-fried yucca blossoms (see page 108) or *papas bravas* (fried potatoes).

Makes 3 quarts (3 liters)

½ cup (120 ml)	extra virgin olive oil
7	serrano peppers, chopped
3	habanero peppers (optional), halved
1	large white onion, chopped
8	garlic cloves, chopped
2 tbsp	dried Mexican oregano
1 tsp	ground cumin
	Kosher (flaked) salt and freshly ground black pepper
12 cups (3 liters)	canned peeled whole San Marzano tomatoes (one #10 can, or three 35 oz/992 g cans)

In a large saucepot, heat the olive oil over medium heat. Add the serranos, habaneros, onion, and garlic and cook until softened but not browned, about 6 minutes. Add the oregano and cumin. Season with a little salt and black pepper. Add the tomatoes and bring to a simmer. Stir occasionally and cook until most of the residual water has evaporated, about 15 minutes.

Allow to cool for 1 hour. Working in batches, puree the sauce in a high-powered blender. Adjust the seasoning with salt and black pepper. Serve hot or refrigerate for up to 5 days.

Pepita Vinaigrette

THE SEEDS OF SQUASH AND pumpkins were an original food source for fat and flavor for the people of the Americas. Many types of squash also became drinking gourds and other utilitarian vessels. We make vinaigrette out of the pumpkin seeds, which give it a vibrant green color and complex, nutty flavor.

Makes 1 cup (240 ml)

2 cups (260 g)	hulled pumpkin seeds
½ cup (10 g)	chopped parsley leaves
1 cup (240 ml)	fresh lemon juice
½ cup (120 ml)	unpasteurized organic apple cider vinegar
3 cups (710 ml)	extra virgin olive oil
	Diamond Crystal kosher (flaked) salt and freshly ground black pepper

On a comal or in a dry frying pan, toast 1 cup (130 g) of the pumpkin seeds until lightly browned and fragrant. Let cool to room temperature. Transfer the toasted pumpkin seeds to a food processor and add the remaining 1 cup (130 g) seeds, the parsley, lemon juice, and vinegar and puree. With the machine running, slowly add the olive oil to emulsify. Season with salt and pepper to taste.

Pico de Gallo

PICO DE GALLO LITERALLY TRANSLATES as "beak of the rooster," because the size that the ingredients are cut into is small enough for a rooster to pick up individually with his beak. Traditionally it is made with tomato, but we omit the tomato and use red onions instead of white. When I first spent a few months in Mexico when I was nineteen years old, the mama at the house I stayed in made chicken soup once a week and served it with spicy *pico de gallo*, no tomato, and lime so I have grown to prefer this simple salsa prepared this way.

Makes 1 cup (240 ml)

2	red onions, cut into ⅛-inch (3 mm) dice
4	jalapeños, seeded and cut into ⅛-inch (3 mm) dice
1 bunch	cilantro (fresh coriander), finely chopped
½ cup (120 ml)	fresh lime juice
¼ cup (60 ml)	extra virgin olive oil
½ tsp	ground allspice
½ tsp	ground cumin
	Diamond Crystal kosher (flaked) salt and freshly ground black pepper

In a bowl, combine the onions, jalapeños, cilantro (fresh coriander), lime juice, olive oil, allspice, cumin, and salt and black pepper to taste. Let sit for 1 hour, then adjust the seasoning if necessary. Serve immediately.

Salsa de Chapulines

COMBINING THE NORMAL INGREDIENTS FOR salsa with a small amount of *chapulines* in a volcanic molcajete creates a darker, more complex salsa that can be paired with anything you would pair the normal salsa with. My favorite way to eat it is with fresh, steaming hot, almost paper-thin blue tortillas and a Michelada.

Makes 1 cup (240 ml)

2	red tomatoes, cut into medium dice
½	large white onion, cut into medium dice
2	jalapeños, seeded and finely diced
4 tbsp	chapulines (dried grasshoppers), toasted
½ cup (10 g)	cilantro (fresh coriander) leaves, chopped
¼ cup (60 ml)	fresh lime juice
	Sal de Chapulín (page 202), sal de gusano, or kosher (flaked) salt
	Freshly ground black pepper

In a molcajete or large mortar and pestle, combine the tomatoes, onions, jalapeños, *chapulines*, cilantro (fresh coriander), lime juice, and salt to taste. Process with the *mano* or in a food processor until you have a cohesive but still slightly chunky salsa. Season with pepper. Store in an airtight container in the refrigerator for up to 5 days.

Salsa Fresca

SIMILAR TO *PICO DE GALLO* in terms of ingredients, we add tomato to this salsa and cut the ingredients into bigger pieces. The simplest and most universally appealing salsa pairs with anything and is best served with fresh fried corn chips or nachos.

Makes 6 cups (1.4 liters)

4	large red tomatoes, cut into ¼-inch (6 mm) dice
1	large white onion, cut into ⅛-inch (3 mm) dice
4	jalapeños, seeded and cut into ⅛-inch (3 mm) dice
½ cup (10 g)	parsley leaves, chopped
1 bunch	cilantro (fresh coriander), finely chopped
½ cup (120 ml)	fresh lime juice
¼ cup (60 ml)	fresh lemon juice
¼ cup (60 ml)	extra virgin olive oil
½ tsp	ground cumin
	Kosher (flaked) salt and freshly ground black pepper to taste

In a large bowl, combine all the ingredients and let sit for 1 hour. Taste and adjust the seasoning if necessary. Serve immediately.

Salsa Pasilla

SALSA PASILLA IS A VERY traditional salsa preparation from Mexico. In our version, we brighten it up and sweeten it a little bit with fresh orange juice and sometimes substitute grapefruit, satsumas, or tangerines if they are in season and particularly vibrant. It is flavorful but mild in terms of chile heat and pairs well with hot tortillas and roasted meats. We serve it with our ancho chile relleno.

Makes 1 cup (240 ml)

12	dried pasilla chiles
8	ancho chiles
	Boiling water
5	garlic cloves, peeled
2 cups (475 ml)	fresh orange juice
	Kosher (flaked) salt

On a hot comal or in a dry frying pan, toast the pasillas and the anchos until fragrant. Remove the stems and the seeds. Transfer the chiles to a heatproof bowl. Cover with boiling water and let soak for 1 hour.

Reserving the soaking liquid, drain the chiles and transfer them to a blender. Add the garlic, orange juice, and some of the soaking liquid to make it into a thick sauce or light paste. Season with salt to taste. Serve immediately.

Squash Leaf, Radish Top, or Beet Green Pesto

WE ARE ALWAYS TRYING TO use the tops and leaves of plants and sneak a vegetable into people's lives out here in the desert. Bettina came up with using any one of these to make our version of pesto. We serve it with boquerones, masa pasta, or simply roasted carrots.

Makes 1 quart (1 liter)

1½ cups (195 g)	hulled pumpkin seeds
2 qt (2 liters)	firmly packed greens, stemmed and washed
1 tsp	citric acid
2 cups (475 ml)	extra virgin olive oil
	Kosher (flaked) salt and freshly ground black pepper

On a hot comal or in a dry frying pan, toast 1 cup (130 g) of the pumpkin seeds until lightly toasted and fragrant. Let cool, then transfer to a food processor. Add the remaining ½ cup (65 g) pumpkin seeds, the greens, and citric acid and puree. With the machine running, slowly add the olive oil to emulsify. Season with salt and pepper to taste.

We freeze the mixture in Pacojet beakers and Pacotize 2 times before serving. This gives the pesto a particularly smooth texture while maintaining the vibrant green color. You can also puree this in a high-powered blender skipping the freezing part and serve immediately or store in an airtight container in the refrigerator for up to 3 days.

Raw Salsa Verde

IN MEXICO, SALSA VERDE IS traditionally made by boiling tomatillos, onions, and chiles and then pureeing those ingredients into salsa. We were trying to imagine a fresher more vibrant version with a more concentrated and less waterlogged taste. A healthy dose of fresh allspice adds a natural sweetness and spice to the acidic tomatillos. Sometimes we even puree an avocado in to add more body to the salsa.

Makes 6 cups (1.4 liters)

2 lb (910 g)	tomatillos, husked and quartered
6	serrano peppers, chopped, seeds left in for spice (optional)
2	jalapeños, seeded and chopped
½	large white onion, cut into chunks
2	garlic cloves, peeled
¼ cup (60 ml)	fresh lime juice
2 tbsp	distilled white vinegar
8	allspice berries, toasted and ground in a mortar or spice grinder
3 tbsp	piloncillo
1 tsp	citric acid (optional)
	Diamond Crystal kosher (flaked) salt and freshly ground black pepper

In a high-powered blender, working in batches if necessary, combine the tomatillos, peppers, onion, garlic, lime juice, vinegar, allspice, sugar, and citric acid (if using). Process on the highest setting. Season to taste with salt and pepper. Store in an airtight container in the refrigerator for up to 5 days.

Recado Negro

RECADO NEGRO IS YUCATECAN IN origin and possibly the mother of all moles. Traditionally the ingredients are all indigenous and roasted until black. Depending on the chiles it can be as spicy as you like. It can also be thick or thin, hot or cold, used as seasoning, stuffing, sauce, or salsa. This versatility and heat led us to create our own riff on the traditional recipes.

Makes 1 quart (1 liter)

1 lb (500 g)	corn tortillas, homemade (see page 162) or store-bought
5½ oz (160 g)	dried árbol chiles
5½ oz (160 g)	dried guajillo chiles
5½ oz (160 g)	ancho chiles
3	dried chipotle peppers
	Boiling water, for soaking
2½ tbsp	black peppercorns
2½ tbsp	dried Mexican oregano
2½ tbsp	cumin seeds
12	whole cloves
12	allspice berries
15	garlic cloves, peeled
1	large white onion, roughly chopped

On a hot comal or in a dry frying pan, cook the tortillas on both sides until they are blackened, dry, and crispy.

On the comal or in the frying pan, toast the 4 chile varieties until they are blackened, about 8 minutes. Remove the stems and the seeds and transfer the chiles to a heatproof bowl. Cover with boiling water and let soak for 1 hour.

On the comal or in the frying pan, toast the remaining ingredients until they are blackened.

Reserving the soaking water, drain the chiles. Transfer the chiles to a high-powered blender, break up and add the tortillas, toasted spices and herbs, garlic, and onion and blend to make a smooth black paste, using the reserved chile soaking water to adjust the consistency to a thick-bodied salsa. (Alternatively, grind everything together on a metate.) Store in an airtight container in the refrigerator for up to 3 months.

Salsa Huitlacoche

HUITLACOCHE IS A DELICACY AND it's best when prepared from freshly picked ears of corn. That being said, it is also technically a plant disease: A pathogenic fungus causes the corn it affects to grow large, black, misshapen bulbous nodules where the kernels should have been. It is indeed edible, highly prized, and very delicious. We make a salsa out of it and serve it with our duck dishes.

Makes 1 quart (1 liter)

3	serrano peppers
1	large white onion, unpeeled
1 head	garlic, unpeeled
4 tbsp	lard or avocado oil
1 jar (32 oz/ 907 g)	huitlacoche, drained
½ cup (120 ml)	homemade duck jus reduction or store-bought demi-glace (optional)
	Kosher (flaked) salt and freshly ground black pepper

On a hot comal or in a dry frying pan, toast the serranos, onion, and garlic whole until lightly charred on the outside, about 10 minutes. Allow to cool and then peel each and roughly chop.

In a frying pan, heat the lard over medium-high heat. Add the huitlacoche and the chopped serranos, onion, and garlic and cook until the onion is softened but not browned, about 10 minutes. Transfer the mixture to a high-powered blender and puree. Season to taste with duck jus reduction (if using), salt, and pepper. Serve immediately.

Fermented Red Sauce

WE HAD BEEN DOING A lot of fermenting projects and realized we wanted to make fermented salsas as well. The original inspiration was for developing complexity of flavor, and that fermented chiles are healthier and more digestible for certain people. We forgot about the chiles when one of our chefs decided to use plums from our orchard instead, lending sweetness and balance to the fermented salsa. They are also fun to eat cold with a sip of mezcal.

Makes 1 quart (1 liter)

1 lb 2 oz (500 g)	Mezcal-Poached Plums (recipe follows), halved and pitted
1 lb (450 g)	Mak Kimchi (page 226)
¼ cup (60 ml)	agave syrup
	Kosher (flaked) salt

In a high-powered blender, combine the plums, kimchi, agave syrup, and salt to taste and puree. Transfer to a 2-quart (2-liter) container covered with cheesecloth or a loose-fitting lid. Let sit at room temperature for 3 days to ferment. Store airtight in the refrigerator.

MEZCAL-POACHED PLUMS
Makes 8 quarts (8 liters)

4½ lb (2 kg)	purple plums
1 bottle (750 ml)	Del Maguey Vida mezcal
½ cup (120 ml)	agave syrup
2	habanero peppers, halved
1	cinnamon stick
3	bay leaves
4	whole cloves
1 tbsp	cardamom pods
1 tsp	caraway seeds
1 tsp	coriander seeds
½ tsp	ground allspice
1 tsp	dried epazote

In a large pot, combine the plums, mezcal, agave, habaneros, and all the spices and herbs. Bring to a simmer, then remove from the heat. Let the plums cool in the poaching liquid. Store in the refrigerator.

Fermented Green Sauce

THIS FERMENTED GREEN SAUCE BECOMES the counterpoint to our fermented red sauce in our Camarones Divorciado (page 118) and mimicks the traditional Mexican dish while being our own interpretation.

Makes 1 quart (1 liter)

4	habanero peppers, halved
10	peaches, pitted and finely diced
1	small bunch garlic chives, chopped
1 cup (60 g)	packed shiso leaves, chopped
	Leaves from 3 Mexican oregano sprigs, chopped
2 tbsp	chopped fresh epazote
1	white onion, finely diced
5 tbsp	kosher (flaked) salt
1	vanilla bean, split lengthwise

In a bowl, toss together all the ingredients to evenly distribute the salt. Firmly pack all the ingredients into a 1-quart (1-liter) jar or container. Let sit covered with a loose lid or cheesecloth at room temperature for 3 days to ferment. Remove the vanilla pod. Transfer the mixture to a high-powered blender and puree. Store in an airtight container in the refrigerator.

Catclaw Honey and Lime Vinaigrette

OUR FRIEND JONNY SUFFICOOL PROVIDES us with honey that comes from bees that feed predominantly on the nectar from the catclaw acacia that grows in the Southwest. This honey is mild in flavor and popular among tea drinkers. The catclaw honey that Jonny brings is clear when liquid and snow white when crystallized. It is rumored to contain more antioxidants and anti-inflammatory properties than other honeys. Any mild or local honey can be easily substituted.

Makes about 5 cups (1.2 liters)

½ cup (120 ml)	unpasteurized apple cider vinegar
¼ cup (60 ml)	rice vinegar
½ cup (120 ml)	fresh lime juice
¼ cup (85 g)	catclaw honey
2 tbsp	Dijon mustard
1	egg yolk
2	shallots, minced
1	garlic clove, minced (optional)
3 cups (710 ml)	extra virgin olive oil
	Salt and freshly ground black pepper

In a blender or food processor, combine the vinegars, lime juice, honey, mustard, egg yolk, shallots, and garlic (if using). Process to a puree. With the machine running, slowly add the olive oil to emulsify. Season with salt and pepper to taste. Refrigerate until ready to use. If left out, the emulsion will break.

Marigold Variation: Add 2 cups (120 g) marigold petals to the puree.

Tamarindo Variation: Replace the catclaw honey with tamarind concentrate.

Pomegranate Variation: Replace the catclaw honey with pomegranate molasses.

Pickles and
Ferments

The seeming lack of fresh produce in the area was one of several key points of inspiration for me in my current commitment to a lifetime of learning about the inhabitants and the culture (most importantly what they ate) of our specific region, and more broadly the Americas.

Yucca Jam

THIS YUCCA JAM WAS ORIGINALLY created as a base layer in our Seven-Layer Yucca Dip (page 88) but we also like to smear it on toast with something savory like foie gras or anchovies or even pureed olives for a snack.

Makes 1 quart (1 liter)

2 lb (950 g)	yucca blossoms
4 cups (800 g)	sugar
¼ cup (60 ml)	fresh lemon juice
5	allspice berries
1	Ceylon cinnamon stick

In a heavy-bottomed nonreactive pot, combine 4 cups (1 liter) water, the yucca blossoms, sugar, lemon juice, allspice, and cinnamon stick. Bring to a boil. Reduce the heat to a slow simmer and cook, stirring periodically, until the water has evaporated and the mixture has thickened, feels jammy, or coats the back of a spoon. Remove from the heat and cool to room temperature. Remove the spices. Use immediately or transfer the jam to a jar or other airtight container and store in the refrigerator for up to 8 weeks.

Pickled Yucca Blossoms and Buds

Makes 1 quart (1 liter)

1 lb (500 g)	yucca flowers and/or buds
½ oz (10 g)	fresh ginger, sliced
1 tbsp (12 g)	sugar
3 cups (700 ml)	unpasteurized apple cider vinegar
2 cups (475 ml)	white wine

Place the yucca flowers in a heatproof bowl. In a nonreactive pot, combine the ginger, sugar, vinegar, and white wine. Bring to a boil and pour over the yucca flowers. Let cool. Refrigerate in an airtight container for 2 weeks before serving.

Fermented Yucca Buds and Flowers

WE USE THESE FERMENTED YUCCA buds in our Seven-layer yucca dip (page 88), and sometimes skewer them with an anchovy and an olive as a garnish for our own version of Death & Co.'s Gilda cocktail.

Makes 1 quart (1 liter)

2 tbsp (30 g)	kosher (flaked) salt
2 lb 3 oz (1 kg)	yucca flowers, petals only (stems and stamens removed)
2 lb 3 oz (1 kg)	yucca buds, stems removed

In a nonreactive bowl, sprinkle the salt over the yucca petals. Massage with your hands. Cover and let sit for 2 hours at room temperature. Vacuum-seal the petals and buds and any liquid collected in the bowl and let sit at room temperature for 3–4 days until it smells pleasantly fermented. Refrigerate in the vacuum bag.

Pickled Chayote Squash

CHAYOTE IS ONE OF SEVERAL foods introduced to the Old World during the Spanish Conquest. I first had this member of the squash family in New Orleans, where they call it mirliton. It is not generally eaten raw, but we developed a pickling recipe that preserves the noble squash's character and dresses it up with some old friends from the *milpa*, which are the chiles. The *milpa* is a Mexican system in which corn, beans, squash, tomatoes, and chiles all grow together in harmony.

Makes 1 quart (1 liter)

2	ancho chiles
6	dried árbol chiles
2	dried pequín chiles
3	chayote squash, peeled, seeded, and cut into 1-inch (2.5 cm) slices
3 tbsp	kosher (flaked) salt
6 tbsp	sugar
3 cups (710 ml)	white wine vinegar
2 cups (475 ml)	unpasteurized apple cider vinegar

In a dry frying pan, toast the chiles until fragrant. In a 2-quart (2-liter) nonreactive container, combine the toasted chiles, squash, salt, sugar, and both vinegars. Cover and refrigerate for at least 3 days before serving.

Pickled Habanero, Jalapeño, or Serrano Peppers

THESE PICKLED CHILES AND THEIR pickling liquid are served on our pickle plate at the restaurant for the humans who, like me, like a dose of heat for a little mouth burn and to get the endorphins going. Although we use the same pickling mix for each chile, we pickle them all separately. The reason for this is that we use each chile for different applications or we use the habanero vinegar as a seasoning on its own. Make sure to wear gloves while you are prepping your chiles!

Makes 2 quarts (2 liters) chiles

1 lb (450 g) total	fresh chiles, such as habaneros, jalapeños, or serranos
5	garlic cloves, crushed
1½ cups (355 ml)	white wine vinegar
1½ cups (355 ml)	apple cider vinegar
1½ cups (300 g)	sugar
3 tbsp	kosher (flaked) salt
3 tbsp	coriander seeds

If you are using habaneros, halve them lengthwise. If you are using jalapeños or serranos, make 2 small slits in each chile using a paring knife. This allows the pickling liquid to penetrate the chiles.

In a 4-quart (4-liter) nonreactive container, combine the chiles, garlic, both vinegars, sugar, salt, and coriander seeds. Cover and refrigerate for at least 3 days before serving.

Cured Egg Yolks

I THOUGHT THE AIR CURED egg yolks were an original idea but later realized lots of people have been doing this which proves that maybe there is nothing new under the sun or even swinging in the breeze. The intent was to mimic bottarga and echo the flavor of our egg yolk ravioli with masa pasta on page 138.

Makes 12 cured egg yolks

2 cups (270 g)	kosher (flaked) salt
1 cup (200 g)	sugar
12	egg yolks, preferably from eggs from your own chickens

In a small bowl, stir together the salt and sugar. Layer half of the mixture in a nonreactive container (we use a square 2-quart/2-liter plastic container with a lid that is 2 inches/5 cm deep) and arrange the egg yolks on the curing mixture spaced at least 1 inch (2.5 cm) apart. Cover them with the other half of the curing mix. Cover the container, place in the refrigerator, and let cure for 7 days.

Remove the yolks and rinse under cool water and place on paper towels to dry. We then tie them in individual sachets of cheesecloth and hang them in a cool breezy place for 3–5 days. We do this to make them very dry so that when we grate them on the Microplane the end result is fluffy, like aged Parmesan cheese. This step is optional. Store in an airtight container.

Pickled Garlic Cloves

ON A WHIM ONE DAY, I put a few pickled garlic cloves on the pickle plate that we serve at the bar, and our guests started demanding the pickled garlic cloves from the pickled chile recipe (opposite), so we started pickling fresh garlic using the prickly pear vinegar that we make in house. We serve them as a snack, use them as a cocktail garnish, or eat them ourselves throughout the long days of cooking.

Makes 2 quarts (2 liters)

2 lb (910 g)	garlic cloves, unpeeled but lightly crushed
5	jalapeño or serrano peppers, sliced
3 cups (710 ml)	distilled white vinegar
1 cup (240 ml)	prickly pear vinegar
1½ cups (300 g)	sugar
1 tbsp	kosher (flaked) salt

In a 2-quart (2-liter) glass jar, combine the garlic, chiles, both vinegars, sugar, and salt. Cover and refrigerate for at least 3 days and up to 6 weeks.

Fresh Pickled Cucumbers

IN THE SUMMER MY GREAT-GRANDMOTHER always had a bowl of fresh cucumbers marinating in salt and distilled white vinegar on the table when we were having lunch and dinner. We like to re-create that for a little nostalgia but substitute rice vinegar and a little Korean chile for spice.

Makes 2 quarts (2 liters)

3 lb (1.35 kg)	English (seedless) or Armenian cucumbers
4 tbsp	kosher (flaked) salt
1 cup (200 g)	sugar
3 cups (710 ml)	rice vinegar
2 tbsp	gochugaru (Korean red chili flakes)

Trim the ends of the cucumbers and, using a mandoline, thinly slice into rounds about ⅛ inch (3 mm) thick. Season both sides of the cucumbers with the salt and allow them to drain on a rack for 30 minutes.

In a saucepan, combine 1 cup (240 ml) water, the sugar, vinegar, and gochugaru and bring to a boil. Let the pickling liquid cool, then submerge the cucumber slices in it. Serve immediately.

Pickled Jicama

FOR A LOT OF OUR pickle recipes we use the refrigerator method in which none of the ingredients are cooked. All you have to do is combine everything and put it in the refrigerator, where the pickles maintain their freshness and integrity. This is especially important for the jicama.

Makes 2 quarts (2 liters)

3	medium to large jicama (yam bean), peeled and cut crosswise into 1-inch (2.5 cm) slices
2 cups (475 ml)	white wine vinegar
2 cups (475 ml)	rice vinegar
1 cup (240 ml)	fresh lime juice
5	serrano peppers, sliced
2 tbsp	kosher (flaked) salt
8-inch (20 cm) piece	fresh ginger, peeled and cut into 1-inch pieces
1 cup (43 g)	dried hibiscus flowers

In a 4-quart (4-liter) nonreactive container, combine the jicama, both vinegars, lime juice, chiles, salt, ginger, and hibiscus flowers. Cover and refrigerate for at least 3 days. To serve, cut the sliced jicama lengthwise again, creating 1- by 1-inch (2.5 × 2.5 cm) matchsticks.

Pickled Quince

BEFORE BETTINA STARTED WORKING AT the Capri, she would come in as a guest and sometimes bring us gifts of things she was making at home. The first thing she ever brought us was a small jar of pickled quince. It was so good that I put it on the menu that night. We continue to make pickled quince when it is in season and have even found a couple of quince trees growing in Marfa. It pairs wonderfully with foie gras, our cheese plate, or rabbit mousse.

Makes 2 quarts (2 liters)

5 lb (2.25 kg)	quince, peeled, cored, and quartered
8 strips (2 × 1 inch/ 5 × 2.5 cm)	lemon zest
8-inch (20 cm) piece	fresh ginger, peeled and sliced
6 tbsp	sugar
3 tbsp	kosher (flaked) salt
2 cups (475 ml)	white wine vinegar
4 tbsp	mirin
2 tsp	juniper berries
2 tsp	agarita berries

In a large nonreactive pot, combine the quince, lemon zest, ginger, sugar, salt, vinegar, juniper, agaritas, and mirin. Bring to a boil and immediately turn off the heat. Let cool, then transfer to a 4-quart (4-liter) container. Cover and refrigerate for 2 weeks before serving.

Pickled Muscat Grapes

WE HAVE A GIANT PERGOLA covered with grapevines. In the summer it is a race against time—and the birds—to get as many grapes as we can. What we don't eat or serve fresh, we like to pickle for later use.

Makes 2 quarts (2 liters)

2 lb (910 g)	Muscat grapes
¾ cup (150 g)	sugar
1 tsp	kosher (flaked) salt
3 tbsp	grated fresh ginger
	Grated zest of 1 lime
	Grated zest of 1 lemon
8	whole cloves
2	green cardamom pods, crushed
1	Mexican cinnamon stick
2	whole star anise

Place the grapes in a heatproof bowl. In a saucepan, combine 1 cup (240 ml) water, the sugar, salt, ginger, citrus zest, cloves, cardamom, cinnamon stick, and star anise. Bring to a boil and pour over the grapes. Cool, then cover and refrigerate for 2 weeks before serving.

Pickled Watermelon Rind

WE USE A LOT OF watermelons in the summer. Coming from the South it only makes sense to me to pickle the rinds, since that is a tradition. We developed a recipe that pairs well with charcuterie, cheeses, or radishes, or they are nice to eat on their own.

Makes 4 quarts (4 liters)

4 cups (950 ml)	white wine vinegar
4 cups (950 ml)	rice vinegar
3 cups (300 g)	sugar
2 strips (2 × 1 inch/ 5 × 2.5 cm)	lemon peel
2	Mexican cinnamon sticks
2	whole star anise
3	vanilla beans
8-inch (20 cm) piece	fresh ginger, peeled and cut into 1-inch (2.5 cm) pieces
5 lb (2.25 kg)	watermelon rind, peel removed, cut into 1-inch (2.5 cm) cubes

In a large pot, combine the vinegars, sugar, lemon peel, cinnamon, star anise, vanilla beans, and ginger. Bring to a simmer and cook for 10 minutes. Add the watermelon rind and bring to a boil for 1 minute. Remove from the heat and allow to cool. Transfer everything to a 6-quart (5.6-liter) storage container. Cover and refrigerate at least overnight before serving.

Curtido

CURTIDO IS LIKE CENTRAL AMERICAN sauerkraut. It's mostly used in Salvadoran cuisine, but there is a version in Belize that uses habaneros and vinegar as well.

Makes 4 quarts (4 liters)

3	heads green (white) cabbage, quartered, cored, and thinly sliced
5	carrots, grated on a box grater
3	jalapeños, halved, seeded, and thinly sliced
1	white onion, thinly sliced
2 tbsp	crushed red pepper flakes
2 tbsp	dried Mexican oregano
½ cup (120 ml)	extra virgin olive oil
	Kosher (flaked) salt

In a large bowl, mix together the cabbage, carrots, jalapeños, onion, pepper flakes, oregano, and olive oil. Take a weight and add 3 tablespoons kosher (flaked) salt for every 1 pound (455 g) of vegetables. Mix everything together. Transfer to a 6-quart (5.6 liter) container (we use square plastic containers) and press firmly down so that there is at least 1 inch (2.5 cm) of liquid sitting on top. Weight the curtido down with a plate and cover with cheesecloth. Allow to ferment at room temperature until it tastes like spicy sauerkraut, 4–5 days, then refrigerate.

Mak Kimchi (Red)

RED KIMCHI IS ONE OF the first fermented foods we started making because: It is definitely influenced by the Americas with the red chile base, we needed to practice our ferment process, and we love to eat kimchi.

Makes 4 quarts (4 liters)

5 lb (2.25 kg)	napa cabbage (Chinese leaf)
¼ cup (35 g)	kosher (flaked) salt
½ cup (80 g)	chopped onion
2 tbsp	chopped garlic
2 tbsp	dried salted shrimp (prawns)
2 tbsp	sugar
1 tbsp	fish sauce
½ cup (130 g)	gochugaru (Korean red chili flakes)
4	scallions (spring onions), green part only, sliced

Trim the cabbage of outer, undesirable leaves and slice lengthwise into sixteenths. Slice those across into about 1½-inch (4 cm) pieces. Mix and massage with salt and let sit for 1 hour.

In a food processor, combine the onion, garlic, dried shrimp, sugar, and fish sauce and pulse until a paste forms.

Fold the gochugaru, scallions (spring onions), and ¼ cup (120 ml) water into the paste mixture.

Drain the cabbage of accumulated liquid, rinse thoroughly, and drain again for 20 minutes. Mix the cabbage with the spice paste. Transfer to a 6-quart (6-liter) container (we use plastic square containers) and press firmly down so that there is at least 1 inch (2.5 cm) of liquid sitting on top. Weight the kimchi down with a plate and cover with cheesecloth. Let ferment at room temperature until slightly bubbly and pleasantly fragrant, 3–4 days, and then refrigerate for up to 6 months.

Baek Kimchi (White)

WHITE KIMCHI COMES FROM THE northern provinces of Korea and is said to be for the elderly and children because of the lack of chile in the recipe, making it milder. We like it for its subtle, nuanced, and clean flavor. We also did a little research and found that the first recipes originated pre-1600 CE, which means the chile had yet to migrate from the Americas to that side of the world. So it makes sense that they wouldn't have included it.

Makes 4 quarts (4 liters)

2	heads napa cabbage (Chinese leaf), about 2½ lb (1.1 kg) each
2¼ cups (335 g)	kosher (flaked) salt
2 oz (55 g)	dried shiitake mushrooms, soaked in hot water to rehydrate, stems removed
5 oz (140 g)	daikon radish, peeled
1	Asian pear, quartered and cored
4	garlic cloves, peeled
1 oz (28 g)	fresh ginger, peeled
4 tbsp	fish sauce
8	scallions (spring onions), white part only, chopped
3 tbsp	kosher (flaked) salt
2 tbsp	sugar
1 piece (8 × 5 inches/ 20 × 12.5 cm)	kelp (dried kombu) seaweed

Halve the cabbages lengthwise, and at the root end, make an incision 3 inches (7.5 cm) long. In a large plastic container, mix 3 cups (710 ml) water and the salt. Immerse the cabbage in the liquid and let sit at room temperature for 12 hours. Rinse the cabbage and drain for 1 hour.

Meanwhile, in a food processor, combine the rehydrated mushrooms, the daikon, Asian pear, garlic, ginger, 2 tablespoons of the fish sauce, and the scallions (spring onions) and pulse until a coarse paste forms. Rub this paste on and between the cabbage leaves while maintaining the shape of the cabbage. Stack tightly in an appropriate size container.

In a large pot, combine 2 quarts (2 liters) water, the salt, sugar, seaweed, and remaining 2 tablespoons fish sauce. Bring to a simmer for 5 minutes. Let the liquid cool, then pour over the cabbage.

Weight the cabbage down so it is submerged in the liquid. Let ferment at room temperature for 3 days. Refrigerate for at least 2 weeks to mature.

Pickled Jamaica (Hibiscus) Eggs

VIRGINIA DREAMS OF ALWAYS HAVING a giant jar of pickled eggs sitting on the Capri bar, like they did in the old-time mercantiles and saloons of Texas. We have a henhouse, so at certain times of the year, when the ladies are producing lots of eggs, we do our best to make this dream come true.

Makes 12 pickled eggs

12	eggs
1 cup (240 ml)	distilled white vinegar
1 cup (200 g)	sugar
1 tbsp	kosher (flaked) salt
1 cup (43 g)	dried hibiscus flowers

Place the eggs in a single layer in a pot and add water to cover by 1 inch (2.5 cm). Bring to a boil and then remove from the heat. Place a lid on the pot and let sit for 12 minutes exactly. Cool the eggs under running tap water and peel.

Place the eggs in a 2-quart container with a lid. Combine the vinegar, sugar, salt, and hibiscus flowers. Add to the eggs. Cover and refrigerate for at least 3 days before serving.

Prickly Pear Wine Fermented with Wild Prickly Pear Yeast

OUR FRIEND JONNY SUFFICOOL—WHOM I also refer to as Dancing Ass Jonny—is our local and national treasure when it comes to all things having to do with self-sufficiency, unconventional lifestyles, and just plain having fun. He taught me how to make prickly pear wine several years ago. Interesting part about that is that he had taught Virginia the same thing fifteen years earlier, so among the three of us we had all the necessary equipment. Jonny is the very best teacher and is exacting about every step of the process, so the results are always perfect. We chose three different patches of prickly pears and monitored them on a daily basis. They all had distinct flavor profiles that stood out in the end result. One Jonny said tasted "tropical" and I called it Beaujolais Nouveau. Another Jonny deemed "smooth" and I labeled it Burgundy. The last was labeled "Jonny thinks it's sour" and we called that the Bordeaux.

Makes 17 quarts (16 liters)

17 qt (16 liters)	fresh prickly pear juice (from about 20 gallons/80 liters fresh fruit)
10 cups (2¼ lb/2 kg)	sugar
3 packets (5 g each)	Montrachet yeast (optional)
3⅓ cups (800 ml)	Wild Prickly Pear Yeast Starter (recipe follows)

In a sterilized 6-gallon (23-liter) glass carboy, combine the prickly pear juice, sugar, yeast (if using), and yeast starter and give it a good stir. Seal with an airlock and leave in a cool dark place for at least 6 weeks, monitoring the water level in the airlock and tasting periodically.

After 6 weeks, siphon the wine into a fresh and sterilized carboy leaving any sediment behind. Taste and check the alcohol levels. If a higher alcohol content is desired, add an additional 2 cups (400 g) sugar and continue fermenting for up to 6 weeks. If using the Montrachet yeast it will usually top out at 13.5% ABV and if using the wild starter it can go as high as 15 to 16% ABV and the yeast will die and the fermentation process will be done. The wine should sit for another week to allow sediment to settle, but any longer on the "lees" will impart a bitter flavor.

When the alcohol level and flavor are to your liking, it is time to transfer the wine to bottles. We use a machine called a Buon Vino Super Jet, which pumps the wine through ultra-fine filters for purity and clarity. You can also siphon and filter through cheesecloth as you bottle. Refrigerate or store the wine in a cool dark place.

WILD PRICKLY PEAR YEAST STARTER
Makes 1 quart (1 liter)

1–2 qt (1–2 liters)	freshly picked prickly pears, unwashed
1 cup (200 g)	sugar
	Distilled, spring, or rainwater

Fill a clean and sterilized 2-quart (2-liter) mason jar with the prickly pears so that there is still room around them for the water. Add the sugar and fill almost to the top with water. Tighten the lid and give it a shake. Loosen the lid to fingertip tight and allow to sit at room temperature for 3 days until effervescent. Refrigerate. When ready to use, simply pour off the amount of liquid starter that you need.

Tepache Fermented with Mexican Elderflower Yeast

WE WERE FIRST INSPIRED TO make tepache from our trips to Mexico, where the slightly fermented beverage is sold all over, from street vendors, to restaurants, to the markets. It's a very simple and traditional process that we have been able to trace back to pre-Columbian times when it is believed that native humans were fermenting this beverage out of corn—well before the European "settlers" claimed to have taught the "savages" how to do this. Our good friend Pascal Baudar, a wildcrafting expert amongst many other amazing skills, introduced us to the simple way of collecting wild yeasts and fermenting without having to join any neurotic beer brewing clubs. He makes hundreds of variations of fermented beverages, fermented foods, and vegan nut cheeses all using about 90 percent wild forged ingredients. We use the tepache for refreshment, making cocktails, and even sorbet.

Makes 3 gallons (11.4 liters)

6	pineapples
8	piloncillo cones (6 oz/170 g each), crushed
2	Mexican cinnamon sticks
12	whole cloves
6	árbol chiles
2½ cups (600 ml)	Mexican Elderflower Yeast Starter (recipe follows)

Peel and core the pineapples, reserving the rind. Juice the pineapples and combine the juice with the rind, 3 quarts (3 liters) water, the piloncillo, cinnamon sticks, cloves, chiles, and elderflower starter. Place in a sterilized bucket fitted with an airlock. Allow to sit at room temperature, tasting every day until the desired level of fermentation is reached, 3–5 days. Siphon off, strain through a chinois or fine-mesh sieve, and refrigerate.

MEXICAN ELDERFLOWER YEAST STARTER
Makes 1 quart (1 liter)

1 cup (200 g)	sugar
3⅓ cups (800 ml)	distilled, spring, or rainwater
10½ oz (300 g)	fresh Mexican elderflowers, picked before it has rained

In a clean, sterilized 2-quart (2-liter) mason jar, combine the sugar, water, and elderflowers. Tighten the lid and give it a shake. Loosen the lid to fingertip tight and allow to sit at room temperature for 3 days until effervescent. Refrigerate and strain when ready to use.

Brazo de
Tamales lo

ROCKY

Biblioteca

Our fundamental aim at the Capri is about respect and
purity of intention. We want to utilize the original building,
showcasing the simple and sturdy craftsmanship that
makes it what it is. We inject our own stylistic identity, paying close attention to our fellow citizens of the Americas,
our community, and visitors alike. We want to find edible
plants and uncover techniques that might have been forgotten or not yet discovered. This book offers snapshots of
the creation of the Capri and some documentation of the
first three years, but I feel like we have only just begun.

Tools

ROCKY'S PLATING ROOM ALTAR

At the Capri we have one very important ritual. That is the building of the altar at the pass where all the plates are finished by a rotating cast of characters. The altar is progressively built throughout the day and then taken apart at the end of service. After cleaning, we rebuild the altar. And the copal always burns.

ANAFRES DE BARRO ROJO

These the clay pots, which hold the fire to heat the comals, were made in Oaxaca by a family of women living out in the countryside. *Barro rojo* means red clay. Although Oaxaca is known for its traditional black clay pottery, these women live in an area where the clay is red.

COMAL

The comal is the flat disk traditionally used to cook tortillas. This is an *anafre de barro rojo* with a comal heating over a fire.

MANOS

"Hands" in English, *manos* are the partner grinding tools used with metates and molcajetes to macerate ingredients. They are of pre-Columbian origin.

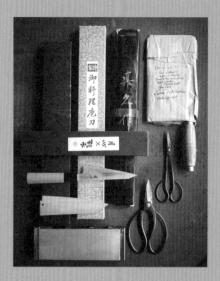

ROCKY'S FAVORITE KITCHEN KNIVES

It seems like we have all started leaning toward using Japanese and Japanese-style knives in the kitchen, so there is quite the selection. There are hand-forged high-carbon steel models, stamped stainless steel, one that was forged from a high-carbon plow blade from the 1920s found out in a field, and even one that was a gift from a guest who had picked up the knife in Hanoi in the 1960s.

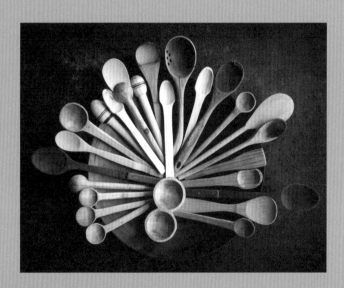

HAND-CARVED SPOONS

We have collected quite the array of spoons over the years and for fun when we serve sorbets and ice creams we like to present the guests with a bowl full of what we call "crazy spoons". This gives the guests options and allows for a little silliness and laughter.

OAXACAN CERAMICS

We use a variety of these red clay ceramics from Oaxaca, both in the kitchen and in the dining room.

Ingredients

ASSORTED MISE EN PLACE FOR SALAD

Top: Hopi amaranth, rosemary blossom, desert marigold
Bottom: Marigold, Mexican elder, honeysuckle.

AGARITA BERRIES AND COLUMBINE FLOWERS

Native berries used for salads, sorbets, and even wild fermented beverages.

HOPI AMARANTH

We use the pods and leaves of this plant for Huauzontles (page 92), and also mix the leaves in to salads, make popcorn out of the seeds, and enjoy watching it grow.

MEXICAN TARRAGON, MEXICAN OREGANO, EPAZOTE

We use this selection of native herbs for everything from salads to ceviche, beans, salsas, and warding off evil spirits.

CARROTS

Grown in our garden to naturally till the land, and also to nourish the staff with a vegetable in whole or juice form. The tops make excellent chimichurri.

RED TRUMPET VINE

Delicate and succulent, Red Trumpet Vine is wonderful mixed into salads or used as a tostada topper.

HUMMINGBIRD BUSH

Hummingbird bush is like tiny red honeysuckle, and is a major part of our functional and flavorful flower garnishes. It can be used sparingly on anything that needs a little feminine sweetness.

MARIGOLD FLOWERS

The spirits of the dead visit the living during the Day of the Dead. Marigolds guide the spirits to their altars using their vibrant colors and pungent scent. Marigolds also represent the fragility of life and pair well with huitlacoche.

MEXICAN ELDERBERRIES AND FLOWERS

Mexican Elder is abundant in our gardens and grows all around us. We like to collect the flowers to make wild yeast starters for our own wines, and even make sodas and syrups from the berries.

MESQUITE BEANS

Collected from a handful of specific trees around us, these pods and their beans are a mainstay flavoring for our bread and our ice cream, and they perfectly represent our desert microcosm.

PRICKLY PEAR CACTUS WITH TUNAS (CACTUS FRUITS)

In the Chihuahuan desert spring the cactus pads become our asparagus and in the fall their fruits become our grapes for making wine.

TURK'S CAP

Another bounteous plant, which produces beautiful sweet flowers and tiny fruits that taste like miniature apples. They go nicely in nopales salads or mixed with arugula.

THE ASSORTED SALTS WE USE AT THE CAPRI

We like to keep an arsenal of salts for interested guests, or just to jazz dishes up a little differently on a whim.

Community

THE CAPRI IS CONSTANTLY UPLIFTED by a community of individuals who bring their expertise to the layers of details that create the whole of the experience at the restaurant. They are the characters that comprise the always-unfolding narrative of the Capri. They are our co-conspirators, our family. They are the ones that lend their support, take issue when it needs to be taken, and listen to us rattle on endlessly about things we don't understand. These people put meat on the bones of any endeavor we undertake. They share their ideas, their resources, and their hard work to imagine and realize the reality of the Capri. We all come together through thick and thin to give this beautiful property its soul, and to create a place for human gathering of which we can be proud.

Sean Daly
COLLABORATOR/DESIGNER/FAMILY

Sean Daly is the Creative Director and designer of the Capri, but so much more. He a weaver of visual tales, the stories that give a space a soul. Every inch of the Capri—every object, textile, glass, table, and stool—has a story inherent in it. You can feel the richness and depth of those stories the minute you walk through the door of the restaurant. Those objects with history give weight to the air. People passing through ask if the restaurant has been there forever, and Sean is to thank for that. When we work together, we are weaving new memories and new experiences into a friendship that gets more textured with every idea. We search for the right visual language, the perfect symbols to tell the story. It's the best to work with someone when it requires few words. To this day Sean travels in and out of Marfa to add layers of new ideas to the design, or to style the space for photo shoots. He is integral to the day-to-day function of the Capri, even from a distance.

— VIRGINIA

Vicente Celis
COLLABORATOR/FAMILY

Vicente makes the world go around as far as we are concerned. He is family. When I first met Vicente I was twenty-two years old. He was working with a dear friend of mine, the artist Michael Tracy, in his hometown of Guanajuato, Mexico. There he was managing a wild array of projects for Michael. He was overseeing the bronzing of sculptures, furniture fabrication, the weaving of rugs, and film production. With the advent of the Capri, Vicente became the head of research and development as we explored the materials and the artisans that tie us symbolically and physically to our incredible neighbor Mexico. He thrives on the madness we create. He is always game when we call at ten o'clock at night to suggest we should drive fifteen hours to central Mexico the next morning to talk to a rug maker or find the artisans working with wooden tools for the kitchen. He sometimes laughs, but he hardly bats an eye. He always says, "Okay, let's do it." Vicente is the magician who can pull a rabbit out of a hat.

—VIRGINIA AND ROCKY

Jon Sufficool
MENTOR

I met Jon Sufficool twenty years ago in Terlingua, a ghost town in South Brewster County. The first summer I knew him, he took me under his wing to teach me the process of fermenting prickly pear wine, from start to finish. If the Capri has a beating heart, it's Jon. He constantly imparts his wisdom of the desert plants and processes he has learned over the years to ignite their medicinal and culinary uses. He is an intrepid outlier never ceasing to explore the knowledge it requires to live off the plants that surround him in the landscape. He is a trader, a giver of gifts, a master refurbisher, a car collector, a wild man with incredible style who dances harder and knows more about the land he lives on than anyone else I have ever known. He is the most photographed man in West Texas. Jon never runs out of stories or knowledge to share. When he comes around, we set everything aside no matter how pressing it might be. We sit and we listen. We never want to miss a word of it.

—VIRGINIA

Jeff Keeling
CAPRI BOTANIST

Jeff is a botanist extraordinaire. He is a professor of applied plant sciences at Sul Ross State University, thirty miles away in the next town over, Alpine. We have a full botanical garden on the Capri property. It boasts over four hundred native species from the American Southwest and northern Mexico, and was originally designed by the brilliant landscape architect Christy Ten Eyck. Jeff has been taking care of these gardens since 2012, and he cares for them as one would care for a child. The native plants are Jeff's passion and in addition to maintaining the gardens, he often takes us out on research and foraging trips at Virginia's mother's ranch. We travel by dune buggy, typically getting stuck a time or two, traversing the desert and always hoping to find something new and fascinating to add to the garden or the kitchen, to deepen the offerings at the Capri. Without Jeff's persistent and kind care, the Capri garden would be a shadow of itself. It is the real magic of this property and restaurant, and it is all thanks to Jeff. It is really his garden.

—ROCKY

Lalo Baeza
GARDENER

Lalo is the tranquil constant gardener who keeps us all calmed down. He just laughs and says, "don't worry, everything is okay." He is the person our dog Tiny loves the most. He feeds our turtle grasshoppers and escargot when we are away. Most importantly, he manages the ancillary gardens at our house that help supply the Capri kitchen. I met Lalo when we first arrived in Marfa, and it always seemed to me that he quietly managed all the most beautiful gardens in town. He was raised in a village called Redford, just on the Texas side of the border, and grew up working on the cantaloupe farms. Lalo cares for plants with a rhythm that feels like meditation. That methodical repetition is how he has become the master of growing the healthiest, most vibrant gardens. Rosa, his wife, is one of the most graceful women in Marfa. We look up to them both as examples of who we hope to become—kind, patient and always elegant.

—VIRGINIA AND ROCKY

Jerram Rojo
BARTENDER

To understand Jerram's role in the front-of-house team at the Capri, all you need to know is that he was the quarterback of his Marfa High School football team. (We are in Texas. There has to be a football reference.) That's exactly how he runs the bar and front-of-house. Jerram was born and raised in Marfa, a local boy through and through. He has been behind the bar since the day we opened. It wouldn't be far-fetched to say we have grown together on this property and learned this business side by side. He knows all the quirks, failings and victories of this establishment. He knows the tender spots and the herculean strengths. He welcomes everyone as a guest. He handles potentially sticky situations with utter wisdom and calm—minus the rare occasion when he runs into the plating room to scream "FUCK IT!" in order to let off a little steam if there is a particularly challenging situation. The Capri is Jerram's, just as much as it is ours. People always tell us that when Jerram isn't at the restaurant, it just doesn't feel the same.

—VIRGINIA AND ROCKY

Joel Hernandez
DISHWASHER

While I was taught in a management class in culinary school that the role of dishwasher is arguably the most important in the house, I learned through working in restaurants that the dishwasher was in fact the most important person in the house. This lesson was impressed upon me during our first few months of the Capri when we were desperately searching for a person that could fulfill this role. How blessed I was to walk in one day and meet Joel Hernandez, who had come to apply for a job. I don't think he ever even touched the application. Although Joel was in high school, he had worked in his parent's restaurant, and came to us with an incredible work ethic and a very mature and respectful demeanor. Just his presence helps keep me calm, and if I start to slip he is not afraid to take me outside and give me a stern talking to. He can fill in as a cook, makes incredible desserts, and can always DJ the party while schooling everyone on music old and new.

—ROCKY

Bettina Landgrebe
ROCKY'S RIGHT HAND IN THE KITCHEN

Bettina Landgrebe, at the time of writing, has been working at the Capri for 2½ years. She is one of the toughest, strongest and most intelligent humans I have ever known. She epitomizes the term "German efficiency," is always on time, and suffers no fools. Before she started working at the Capri, and well before the Capri opening, I met her at a small dinner party I threw. It was on a Tuesday because there were no restaurants open and I felt like cooking, so I sent out an open invitation. At that time I knew her as the only person that would ever return a lent cookbook, which commands respect. In the first year of the Capri, she would come to eat at the restaurant and would also stop by bringing gifts of Sauerkraut or pickled quince that she made for us to try. These items would inevitably wind up on the menu and little did I know at the time that she would inevitably wind up in the kitchen with me. By profession she is a conservator; by passion a very fine cook; and I consider her to be an artist but she would never accept any label that she considered having a hint of pretentiousness.

—ROCKY

Jesús Saenz
SUPPLIER

One day I saw Virginia had written on a piece of paper "Jesus seems to have materialized out of thin air." At first, I was worried that she might have become a born-again Christian. Then I had a laugh because I realized that she was trying to describe our friend Jesús Saenz, and his role in our life. I consider him to be an industrious steward of the land and the culture between the vast expanses of Texas and across the border. He hauls pecan, mesquite, and oak wood to Marfa where he splits and seasons it perfectly. He delivers the best to us and stacks it flusher than the finest brick mason. Jesús also travels from Presidio County down to Chihuahua City stopping everywhere there are small producers of honey, pecans, and Mennonite cheese, and always brings the choicest products to us. He brings us whole honey combs still in the wooden slats they pull from the hives, and although he doesn't drink he has been known to have a bottle of mezcal with a rattlesnake in it for sale if anyone ever thought that would taste good.

—ROCKY

Allan McClane and Malinda Beeman
SUPPLIERS, MARFA MAID DAIRY

Like most people in Marfa, Malinda and Allan always engage in multiple iterations of life simultaneously. Collectively, they have been the founders of Marfa Studio of Arts, co-collaborators in starting Marfa Farm Stand, volunteer firefighters, motorcycle collectors, and builders. Now they are substantially focused on raising their goats and making locally produced cheeses. In Marfa, besides Wilburn the honey man, they were some of the first people to engage in any kind of artisanal culinary endeavors. "Locally made" is not a label one saw often in Marfa. It was a game-changer for our community. I remember the first time I tasted their cheese and saw on the label, "Marfa Made," I thought, "My God we are finally headed down the path to civility!" We are deeply grateful for their dedication. It is not easy. It takes a lot of work. And at the Capri we are lucky to all reap the benefits of serving a cheese that tastes like all the good things in the desert, a cheese that tastes like home.

—VIRGINIA

Rocky's Sketchbook

BOXING DAY

BOUF BOURGUIGNONE (SIC)
CRAB CAKES
BEET SLAW

QUESO
WINGS
CHIX+BEEF PICADO
SANDWICHES

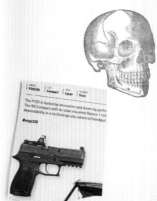

CHIHUAHUAN "SUSHI"

SUSHI RICE (WANTS:
PERSIMMON VINEGAR (3ᴿᴰ)
UME
KELP WRAPPER

TO QUINOA
TO SMELL
TO SMILE
TO OOOOOOOO
AND SOMETHING TO DRINK....

FLOR DE CALABAZA
HUAZONTLES
VERDOLAGA
NOPALES (NERA-NERA)
HONGOS
HUEVOS
JAMAICA
COCONUT OIL (PAROTIZED)
AMARANTH
QUINOA (SPROUTED?)
CHIA (PLEASE!!!)
NAMA SHOYU
SMASHED CUCUMBERS
PICKLED TURNIPS
ANTS
PINE POLLEN
ALGAE
CANYON DAISY
RAICILLA

SUSHI VINEGAR

710 mL RICE VIN
100 G SALT
100 G SUGAR

BLACK BEAN "SOY SAUCE"

FRIJOLES NEGROS (LACTO FERMENT)
HONGOS
DAIKON JUICE   18% SALINITY
BALSAMIC #7 (PASTEURIZE PORQUE)

STACKED PRESSED BAGS

SOUS APPLE (ATV)

PRESSURE CAUSES CLOUDINESS
GRAVITY IS CLARITY
DAILY VERNACULAR
METAL TIN

Jornathan Strange
and Mr Norrel (sic)

CHANCACAS — BLACK AGAVE + SOLIDIFIED
[TECPANCALTZIN] SUGAR (PILONCILLO?)

JEFFREY KEELING

* TIGRIDIA PAVONIA (OCELOXOCHITL O CACOMITL)

* DAHLIA COCCINEA, PINNATA, LEHMANII

* USTILAGO MAYDIS — HUITLACOCHE

* SPIRULINA GEITLERI

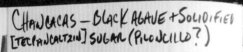

ROCKY (TURKEY, DUCK, DOG, BEE

* ROAST MAGUEY — HOT ROCKS

* WE PAVE THE ROADS OF SHELLS OF HATCHED FOWL

* MOTECUHZOMA'S ZOO

* TLACATAOLLI (HUMAN STEW)

* HEAD TO TAIL SNAKE BRAISED IN PULQUE

* LAKE SHRIMP (CAMBARUS MONTEZUMAE, CAMBARELLUS)

* AXOLOTLS AND TAD POLES TASTE BETTER THAN MEXICALPIS (ALLOTUS)
        (TOTOLLIN O HUEXOLOTL)

CHILE EN NOGADA

FOIE WALNUT EMULSION
POBLANO CONSOMME
WALNUT MILK SKIN
POMEGRANATE PEARLS

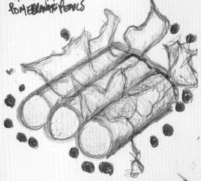

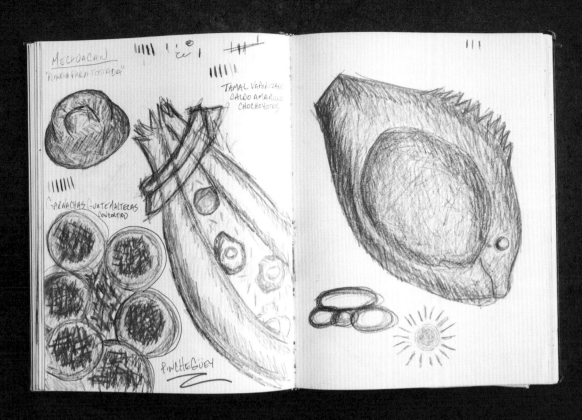
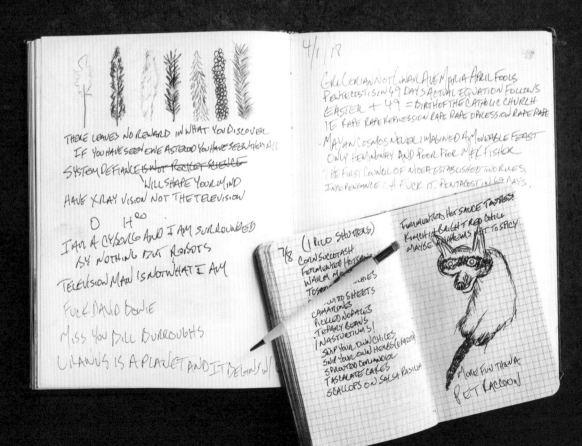

CABEZA DE PERRITA

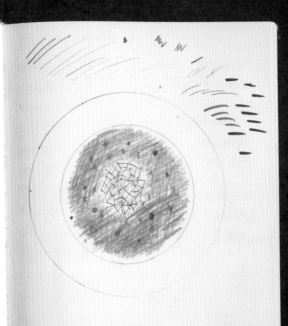

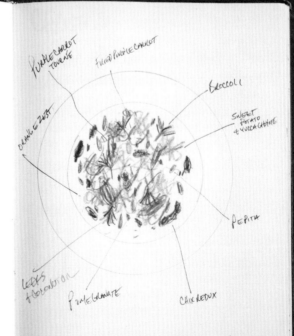

PURPLE CARROT TOURNE

FILLED PURPLE CARROT

BROCCOLI

ORANGE ZEST

SWEET POTATO & YUCCA CHAYOTE

PEPITA

LEEKS & CORIANDER

POMEGRANATE

CHIX REDUX

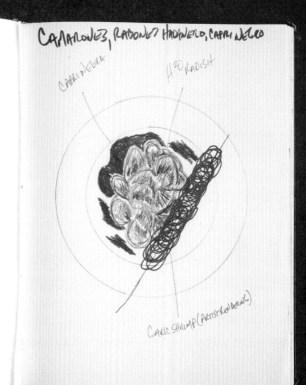

CAMARONES, RADONES HADANELO, CAPRI NEGO

CAPRI NEGRA

H30 RADISH

GARLIC SHRIMP (ARTIST RENDERING)

TRADITIONAL THIRD PERSON =
MOIST TAISTY SNACK CAKE +
VAPID + EPHOMORAL - PROTEIN

NASCENT PLANS
SHEPHERDING PREOCCUPIED
[BRIGHT] YOUNG (MEN)?

OR SOMETHING

Index

Note: Page references in bold indicate photographs.

About the Authors

Virginia Lebermann is from a family of ranchers that has been in Texas for more than a hundred years. She is the co-founder of the Marfa, Texas-based arts organization Ballroom Marfa, and co-owner of the Thunderbird Hotel and the Capri restaurant.

Rocky Barnette is the chef and co-owner of the Capri. He was raised in North Carolina, where he attended culinary school. He worked at the three Michelin-starred Inn at Little Washington in Washington, Virginia for almost a decade before relocating to Marfa, Texas.

Author Acknowledgments

Much gratitude to Sean Daly, who is not only the designer of the Capri, but also our incredible creative director on this book. Thank you always for your creativity, talent, and friendship. Thank you also to Jessica Hundley, our book editor, fearless leader, and friend with impenetrable patience. Thank you for guiding us through this process. Thank you to Douglas Friedman for your stunning photographs for this book, and for your brilliance and warmth of friendship. Thank you to Brian Roettinger for your beautiful design work, and to the Phaidon team for taking a leap of faith. Thank you to Daniel Humm and his team for your kind words and constant inspiration. Huge thanks always to Vicente Celis and to the Capri staff. Thank you also to Brendan Casey and family, Fairfax Dorn, Vance Knowles, Diane Lujan, Las Mujeres de Barro Rojo (Macrena!), and Charlie Hall. Thank you to Donna Lennard for IL Buco, our satellite office. Thank you to Ballroom Marfa for always keeping our lives more vibrant than they would be without you. Thank you to Louise O'Connor, Lowell Lebermann, and to Henry Drake Wotowicz, for all the light and intelligence you bring to all our lives. Thank you to Evelyn Juanita Barnette, F.G. Barnette, Pamela Cook, Robert Heim and to Ed and Anne Ramirez, for taking Rocky in as a feral child and teaching him a little civility. Thank you to Ed Lewis for patiently mentoring and inspiring Rocky as a hyper and difficult high school student, and to Jim "Dutch" Saunders, for teaching Rocky that washing dishes was a viable option if you could not afford to pay for your dinner. Thank you to all of our friends and family in Marfa and beyond who support us always, and to all the musicians and artists that have brought life to the Capri space. And finally, thank you to Boyd Elder, for always protecting us from the pirates and marauders.

Phaidon Press Limited
Regent's Wharf
All Saints Street
London N1 9PA

Phaidon Press Inc.
65 Bleecker Street
New York, NY 10012

phaidon.com

First published 2020
Text © 2020 Virginia Lebermann and
Joseph Rockwell Barnette
Photographs © 2020 by Douglas
Friedman

ISBN 978 18386 6049 9

A CIP catalogue record for this book
is available from the British Library
and the Library of Congress.

Commissioning Editor: Emily Takoudes
Project Editor: Anne Goldberg
Production Controller: Nerissa Vales
Design: Brian Roettinger (WP&A)

Printed in China

The publisher would like to thank
William Norwich, Jessica Hundley,
Daniel Humm, Kate Slate, Linda
Bouchard, and Elizabeth Parson for
their contributions to the book.

Recipe Notes

Unless otherwise noted, salt is Diamond Krystal kosher salt.
The main oils we use are extra virgin olive oil, avocado oil, and
coconut oil, preferably organic.
Many of the recipes call for ingredients that are specific to
the desert region around Marfa, Texas. In most cases, substi-
tutions have not been provided because these ingredients are
integral to the true expression of the dish.